Peter Collins

Fishing the Norfolk Broads

Ernest Benn Limited
London & Tonbridge

Published by
Ernest Benn Limited
25 New Street Square, London, EC4A 3JA
& Sovereign Way, Tonbridge, Kent, TN9 1RW

First edition 1967
Second edition 1970
Third edition (new format) 1977

© Peter Collins 1967, 1977
ISBN 0 510-21003-1
Printed in Great Britain by litho at The Anchor Press Ltd
and bound by Wm Brendon & Son Ltd
both of Tiptree, Essex

The front cover photograph, by Clive Nicholls, shows pike action on Ormesby Broad.

Contents

Publisher's Note 4
Introduction 5
Bank Fishing 9
Boat Fishing 11
Anglers and the Law 13
Broads Fishing Methods 15
River Bure 19
River Ant 33
River Thurne 39
River Yare 43
River Chet 51
River Tas 51
River Waveney 52
River Wensum 61
Wroxham Broad 69
Salhouse Broad 70
Woodbastwick Decoy Broad 72
Hoveton Little Broad 72
Ranworth Maltsters and Inner Broads 73
South Walsham Broads 74
Barton Broad 74
Heigham Sound 76
Hickling Broad 82
Horsey Mere 85
Martham Broad 88
Rockland Broad 89
Oulton Broad 89
Ormesby Broads 92
Fritton Lake 95
Lakes and Pits 97
Fishing Tackle Dealers 99
Fishing Boats for Hire 100
Index 101

Publisher's Note

It is possibly more years than he cares to remember since Peter Collins exchanged his life as a boatbuilder, in the family business at Wroxham, in the heart of Broadland, for a highly successful career in angling journalism. But not before he had gained a great, and perhaps unequalled, all-round knowledge of the Norfolk Broads fisheries. That knowledge was eventually made available to Broads anglers in 1967, when the first edition of this book was published.

Since then a great deal of water has flowed past very many rod tips, and successive new generations of holiday anglers in particular have made good use of the expert advice which this book contains. In this third edition, the text of which has been completely revised, there is an excellent new section on Broads fishing methods, with a number of explanatory illustrations, as well as a collection of maps of the principal fisheries.

The author gratefully acknowledges the assistance given to him by John White, Alan Linstead and Len Bryer, who helped with information on local conditions, and by Ken Clarke, who drew the maps and illustrations.

Introduction

The Norfolk Broads have long been hailed as one of the most prolific coarse fisheries in Britain. There was a time – and not so long ago – when publicists were happy to go a stage further and suggest there was no better fishing anywhere.

The Broads still have enormous potential and contain a fabulous stock of a number of species but there has been a marked decline. That's not to say that locals and visitors alike cannot catch fish in quantity and quality; they can but they need to be more discerning these days.

There are two geographical definitions of the Norfolk Broads. The first is the basically correct one of the Rivers Bure and Yare, with those of their tributaries and associated broads to be found in the navigable waterways below Horstead Mill on the Bure and below Norwich on the Yare. But this is to split hairs. The area visitors have come to know as the Norfolk Broads spreads into Suffolk and extends to the headwaters of all the rivers that eventually flow into the sea at Yarmouth or through Mutford Lock to Lowestoft. For the purposes of this book the title implies the looser definition.

Within the area there are over 500 miles of river and more than 2000 acres of broads – an area in which an angler can find enough to content himself for his lifetime. The basic fish stocks are pike, perch, bream, roach, rudd, tench and dace. Additionally there are eels, smelt, ruffe, and gudgeon; all species with which anglers are not primarily concerned.

A number of other species have been imported into the area with mixed results. Past stocking projects brought in carp, chub, grayling and barbel and of these the great success has been with chub. Introductions were limited to the upper waters of the Bure, Yare and Waveney and the lower section of the Wensum above Norwich.

The only failure was the upper Bure. Everywhere else the chub have thrived, grown and multiplied to the point where outstanding specimens can be caught. Six-pounders have been caught and there is some substance to the

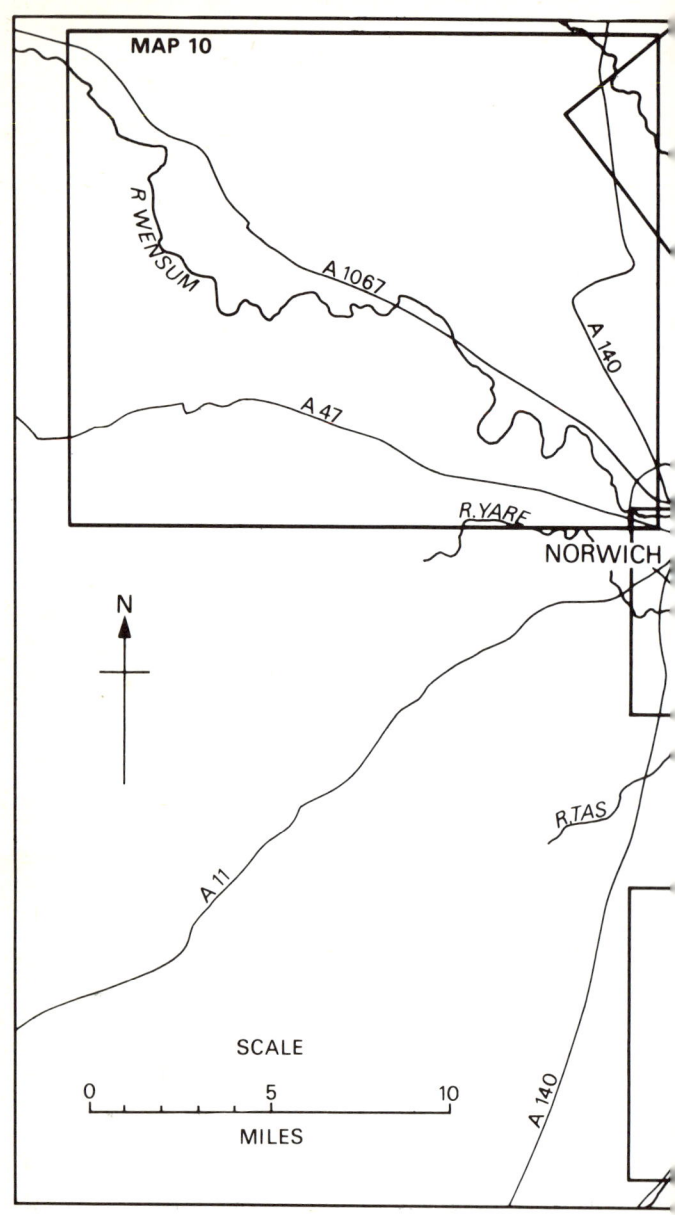

General Map, and Key to Area Maps

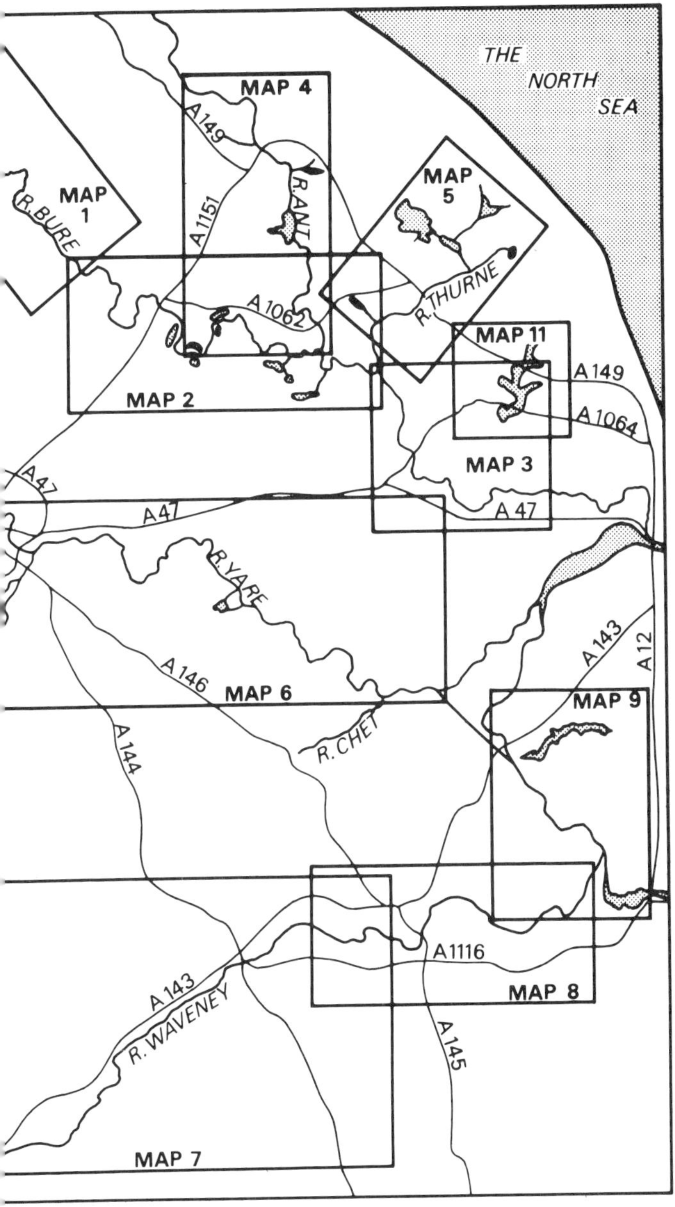
THE
NORTH
SEA
MAP 4
A149
A1151
R.ANT
MAP
1
R.BURE
MAP
5
R.THURNE
A1062
MAP 11
A149
A1064
MAP 2
MAP 3
A47
A47
A47
R.YARE
A143
A12
A146
MAP 6
MAP 9
R.CHET
A144
A1116
MAP 8
A143
R.WAVENEY
A145
MAP 7

thought that there could be national record breakers in Norfolk and Suffolk.

Barbel have also been turned into the Wensum. In all some 200 fish have been released and if that doesn't seem a substantial stocking it is worthwhile remembering that only 509 barbel were released into the River Severn and that river now contains hundreds of thousands of them. There is time for the fish to make an impact here.

Grayling have been a mixed success in the Wensum. It is doubtful if they have done more than maintain their numbers and it is by no means certain they will continue to do even that.

Most of the carp have gone into stillwater fisheries – where they can be expected to produce the best performance – but some were introduced into some of the rivers, a measure which gained the old East Suffolk and Norfolk River Authority no credit marks from me!

Lavish efforts have been made to create trout fisheries in most of the upper rivers and this is also a mixed success, achieved with little regard for its cost.

The popularity of the Norfolk Broads rivers and stillwater systems have contributed to the decline both in the quality and quantity of the fish stock and to the pleasures of catching fish. The incessant river traffic, particularly since the last war when the number of holiday craft began to multiply, has created problems. Weed growth has virtually disappeared in the navigable stretches, the wash from motor cruisers has caused erosion leading to a marked shallowing of all the affected rivers and broads, and fish disease has also made its mark.

In 1967 something like 80 per cent of all the roach died in what proved to be a national catastrophe. In the ten years that have elapsed this situation has largely been corrected – although it must be said by the multiplication ability of the survivors rather than by any efforts by the fishery authority.

Far more serious has been the repeated outbreaks of prymnesium in the headwaters of the Thurne. This was first identified in 1969, although it has perhaps been present for very much longer. Huge quantities of bream, pike, tench and eels died, with the pike and tench losing a greater proportion of their total than other species. Fortunately many of the bream escaped but the loss of pike was enormous and thirty fish on or over the 30lb mark were found dead in one bay of Horsey Mere alone.

Fish of this size cannot be replaced – or replace themselves – overnight and Heigham Sound, Horsey Mere and Hickling Broad are unlikely to be producing big pike in any quantity until 1980 at the earliest.

Pike, of course, exists elsewhere – almost everywhere, in fact, in the system. There is good pike fishing to be enjoyed but we must wait for the very best to re-establish itself.

Perch too have taken a knock from disease and are consequently not so prolific as they used to be. In this instance though there are signs of a general recovery. Quantities of small perch are widespread. Give them time and they will be reaching above the 3lb mark by the early 1980s.

In the main though the stocks of bream have remained untouched. The middle Bure, for example, has a tremendous head of these fish and with the roach also re-established the anglers' bread and butter fish – the ones they come to Norfolk to catch – ensure there are plenty of fish for the catching. Huge catches continue to be made annually throughout most of the river and broads system.

Bank Fishing

Bank fishing within the Norfolk Broads area is exactly the same as fishing anywhere else. Anglers must first have the owner's permission to use his bank or his access to that bank.

Some bank is strictly private. There's no way it can be used. Some is in the hands of local angling organizations and a number of these allow visiting anglers to fish on payment of a daily fee or they invite full membership. Club and association membership fees are usually quite modest and these offer value for money for anglers planning a week's fishing or more in the area.

Fortunately much of the river bank available to anglers is either owned or leased by the Anglian Water Authority, with the fishing controlled and administered by the East Suffolk and Norfolk Division of the Authority.

Throughout the whole area massive lengths of bank are controlled by the Authority, much of it being acquired piecemeal by the now-defunct East Suffolk and Norfolk River Authority and consequently handed on to the Water Authority.

At the time of writing the vast majority of the bank was freely available to all licence holders. Anglers acquire the right to use that bank simply by purchasing a fishing licence. There are, though, some stretches in the upper reaches of the primary rivers where anglers are obliged to obtain a permit in advance from the East Suffolk and

Norfolk Division. These are detailed in this book. Applications should be made to the Fishery Department, East Suffolk and Norfolk River Division, Anglian Water Authority, Yare House, Thorpe Road, Norwich (telephone Norwich 615161).

Unfortunately change is in the air. To offset fishery expenditure which has soared beyond income the Anglian Water Authority plans to apply a scale of charges to anglers fishing from the bank it controls. This may take the form of an annual permit covering all the bank at a fee of perhaps £1. This is being strenuously resisted by local angling organizations and the outcome is not certain. However it may be necessary to obtain one of these bank permits to fish in the 1977/8 season and thereafter. When you buy your normal rod licence for the area ask if these permits are necessary.

There is no continuing guarantee that the bank detailed in this book as available by one means or another will remain open and it is always advisable to check this point. No-one can take for granted permission to fish from any river bank.

There are public staithes in some areas where anglers can fish without charge and many of the boatowners will allow fishing from their bank during the late autumn and winter but again this must not be taken for granted. Ask first, fish later!

Visiting angling clubs are most welcome within the area but they cannot fish competitions without first obtaining the written consent of the Fishery Department of the East Suffolk and Norfolk Division. Clubs must make a written application, advisedly some months in advance, requesting space for a specific number of anglers on the date selected. This has always been a service operated without charge but this too may change and fees may be required. These are not expected to be any more than modest, however.

Once they have obtained permission to use the bank, anglers still have obligations to each other. It is remarkable that a successful angler draws other anglers like a magnet. They will often crowd around him, probably catching nothing themselves and spoiling his sport as well.

There is an unwritten rule among many anglers that they will never fish within twenty yards of anyone else. This is a very good rule indeed and I would like to see it adopted everywhere. To fish one on top of the other spoils everyone's sport – particularly in a flowing river where a man has to work his float tackle downriver with the flow to catch fish.

Boat Fishing

Probably the greatest proportion of anglers who come to the Norfolk Broads to fish intend to do so from a boat. For many of them this will be their first attempt at fishing 'afloat' and there is no reason at all why it should not be an enjoyable experience. There are thousands of boats available of all shapes and sizes — a great many of these are excellent craft, most are at least adequate and only a few are below standard. It is important that anglers should be able to use them to best advantage.

Neither the bigger motor cruisers nor the yachts are satisfactory boats from which to fish. They make excellent mobile living quarters but have many disadvantages so far as fishing is concerned. Far better to fish from the small dinghies that are supplied with most of the holiday craft. These dinghies, usually from 9ft to 14ft in length, can be taken on to shallow areas where bigger boats cannot go. They can be moved quietly without disturbing the fish and they are open to the sky. This leaves anglers with plenty of room to use their fishing tackle unhindered.

Most of these dinghies are equipped with a mast and sail to enable the dinghy to be turned into a small sailing craft. From an angling viewpoint these are unnecessary impediments and are best left back at the boatyard from which the boat was hired. Instead, be sure to obtain two small dropweights for mooring purposes — together with enough rope to allow satisfactory mooring in up to 16ft of water. These can be obtained easily enough on request.

At a great number of boatyards in the area there are also small power-driven launches and rowing boats available for hire on a day-to-day basis. These vary in length, style and quality and everything depends on what they are intended to be used for. The bigger launches — boats up to 18ft long — are ideal for river fishing and for the deeper broads, but care must be exercised when taking these boats on to the shallows of Hickling Broad and Heigham Sound.

When anglers approach a spot they intend to fish, the engine should be switched off while the boat is up to seventy yards away. The noise and disturbance from the motor and propeller can hardly be expected to improve fishing prospects. With the engine switched off, the boat will coast in almost to the required position. A few strokes either with oars or paddles will suffice to bring the boat into exact position.

Mooring should be done quietly and unhurriedly. The weights should not be thrown haphazardly over the side but lowered gently to the bottom. If there are two or more anglers in the boat — when fishing a still water — the boat should be moored square across the wind — not down the wind. Thus all the anglers will have the same chance. Their float tackle will remain still when cast straight out from the boat for the wind is immediately behind them.

Care should be taken to keep well clear of other anglers. There is plenty of space for everyone so there is no point in anglers fishing in a heap!

It pays to approach the final fishing position with the tackle ready for use — put the tackle together while moving towards the swim. It is sensible to remain as still as possible once the fishing position is reached and to make a minimum of noise. Groundbait should already have been wetted and be ready for immediate use.

When moving to another position the mooring weights should be lifted slowly and swilled gently about in the water to remove surplus mud before they are brought aboard. This helps to keep the boat clean and tidy and also prevents accidents. Mud can be very slippery and anyone who steps on some can be sent flying on to the floorboards if he is not careful.

A boat should never be taken through an area where it is intended to fish. This is often done on the shallow water of Heigham Sound and sends the fish scurrying for cover. Anglers then fish for hours on end in areas from which they themselves have thoughtlessly driven away all their sport.

It is illegal to tow fish in a keepnet behind a moving boat. When moving from one spot to another anglers are well advised to return their catches to the water and start again. There is little pleasure in a catch that is killed by ill-treatment. It is also sensible to employ two keepnets if the fish are feeding well — either that or empty the net once it contains a lot of fish and start all over again.

Not all fishing boats are supplied with dropweights for mooring. Some are equipped with two long poles. These should be pressed vertically into the bed of the broad until they are firmly anchored and the mooring ropes are then tied to the tops of the poles. One pole is, of course, used at each end of the boat.

It is best to have a baling tin of some sort in the boat. In the event of rain — or a leak — the water can rise above the floorboards causing discomfort and possibly wet feet. Better to be safe than sorry.

If the boat is hired for the day and has to be rowed any distance the oars must be a balanced pair, complete with leather or wooden stops to prevent the oars from slipping or jumping out of the rowlocks. This is a point to be checked when hiring and any defects which are spotted then can be speedily rectified.

When a fishing boat containing two anglers is being rowed, one man should sit on the middle seat and the other in the stern. If one sits in the bows this makes both steering and progress difficult – if not impossible. It is better for one man to row with both oars rather than for them to have one each. By varying the power used for each stroke the boat can be kept on the right course and when one man has had enough the other can take over for a spell.

On the other hand, an outboard motor will often push a small boat's bows clean out of the water when under way. When this happens it is better for either a man or some of the fishing equipment to be moved into the bows to keep the boat balanced.

When the outboard motor is not in use, it should be protected by a canvas or plastic cover to keep out any moisture. The petrol should, of course, be switched off.

Anglers and the Law

Fishing in the Broads area is controlled by the Anglian Water Authority. This Authority, which came into being in 1974 – replacing the East Suffolk and Norfolk River Authority – is responsible for the maintenance and improvement of the fishing.

The Authority's fishing income is derived from licence sales, the cost of which is generally considered modest in relation to the quality and quantity of the fishing available. The total sales of Norfolk and East Suffolk licences amounts to some £80,000 each year.

An annual licence to fish within the East Suffolk and Norfolk Division costs £1, while a weekly licence costs 40 pence. In addition anglers have the option of purchasing a complete licence to cover the whole of the Anglian Water Authority area, for £2.75. This licence covers Essex, the Great Ouse area, the Welland, the Nene district and Lincolnshire as well as the Broads.

A licence covers only single rod and line. If you plan to use two rods then two licences are needed. An annual trout licence is incorporated in the overall licence. Teenagers of 15 years and older are required to have a licence.

Freshwater fishing licences are on sale in almost every town and village within the wide expanse of Broadland. They cannot be bought from the Authority's fishing bailiffs but are obtainable at tackle shops and a great variety of Post Offices, public houses, general stores and boatyards. Licences can also be bought from tackle dealers in London and many of the provincial towns. Additionally they can be obtained direct from the East Suffolk and Norfolk Division of the Water Authority. Space does not permit the inclusion of the full list of distributors, for they number over 300, but this huge number in itself suggests that no visitor need have difficulty obtaining licences.

In the cause of conservations, by-laws exist which impose a number of sensible restrictions.

The annual close season for freshwater fish is the period between 14 March and 16 June and for trout the period between 30 September and 1 April.

Pike fishing is allowed throughout the whole of the freshwater fishing season, the only restriction being that anglers who livebait before 1 October must catch their bait on the same day they fish for the pike. The reason for this is that it is difficult to keep fish alive in captivity in the warmer months. This stipulation prevents fish from being retained for any undue length of time and thus suffering unnecessary harm.

It is illegal to trail a bait or lure from a moving boat, other than a rowing boat, and only then by using a rod and line. It is also an offence to tow a keepnet containing fish behind a moving boat.

Anglers are not permitted to take away more than two freshwater fish or four trout (excluding migratory trout) in any one day. These fish must all be not less than the following size limits: pike 24in, trout, bream, chub and grayling 10in, carp, tench, perch, roach, rudd and dace 8in.

The written consent of the Authority is needed for club contests in which all fish are to be retained in a keepnet for the weigh-in. These permits — and copies of the full by-laws — are available from the Fishery Department, East Suffolk and Norfolk Division, Anglian Water Authority, Yare House, Thorpe Road, Norwich.

Broads Fishing Methods

Catching fish is easy ... once you know precisely what to do. Yet many visitors fail – simply because they don't adapt their tackle to the water on which it is used. The main causes of failure are in bait presentation and swim feeding. With those faults corrected even anglers of moderate ability can multiply their catches.

The following thirteen points should always be borne in mind:

1. The float should be shotted down so that no more than $\frac{1}{2}$ in of the tip is visible. For short range fishing $\frac{1}{4}$ in above the surface is ample.
2. Match the hook size to the size of the bait. Examples: one maggot equals size 18 or 20 hook, two maggots equals size 16 or 18 hook, with a correspondingly larger hook for additional maggots in the few instances where this is necessary. For bread fishing the hook should be in the size 8 to 14 range – depending on the size of the pieces of the bread being used.
3. The shot used to counterbalance the float should not be placed too close to the hook. See the examples shown in the drawings.
4. The line should fill the spool of your fixed spool reel – to aid easy, accurate casting. And the line should never be too strong. Strength means thickness. Bottom fishing lines should be between 2lb and 3lb breaking strain – there's little need for anything stronger other than for barbel and carp.
5. Never sit too close to another angler. Stay 20 yards away and you give yourself – and the other fellow – a better chance.
6. Don't economize on bait. Two hundred maggots may be enough for one day's hookbait but you need at least a pint, probably two, to keep fish feeding in your swim.
7. Get those feed maggots into your swim with groundbait. Muddy water needs more groundbait than clear water before fish are over-fed.
8. Groundbait should not be made into a stiff 'pudding'. Except where the flow is very strong (on the Bure at Acle, for example) the groundbait should break up on impact with the surface and settle to the bottom in fragments.
9. Never fish in an area where fishing will be interrupted by continuous boat traffic. This applies particularly to areas where the water is less than 6ft deep.

The two extreme types of float show how one carries the buoyancy in its tip and the other has its buoyancy in its base and mid-section. Float A is used to ride flowing water in circumstances where float B would drag under. On the other hand float B is much better in still or slow-moving water since the tip is very fine and is not affected so much by the strength of the wind. Float A would normally be fished fastened top and bottom to the line, whereas float B is fixed at the bottom end only. All floats are variations on these two extremes.

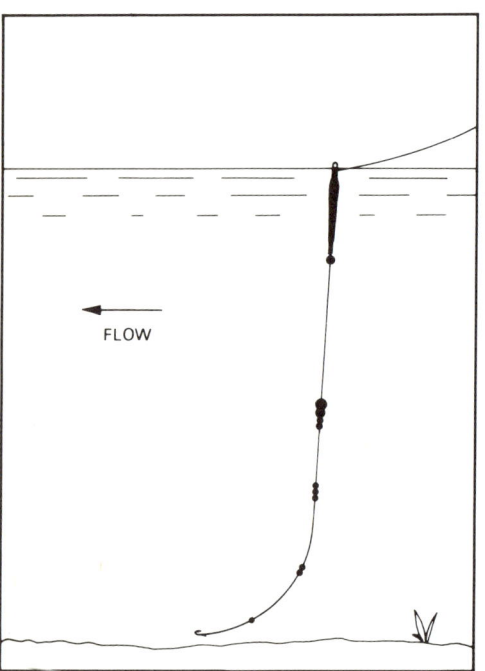

A   B

FLOW

This drawing shows the shot patterns used to fish deep, fast-flowing water, such as the lower Bure. The shot are grouped with the main bunch located at just over half depth. The remainder are located so that the quantity of lead tapers off towards the hook. This helps ensure that the hookbait fishes the bottom of the river and the fish feel minimum resistance as they take the bait.

Experienced anglers don't need to be told right from wrong when shotting a float but many newcomers to angling sample fishing for the very first time when on holiday in Broadland. Here's their first mistake. Float A slides under with ease when a bite comes but the resistance provided by the amount of float above the surface in example B discourages fish. The small lack the strength and the bigger ones the inclination to pull the float down very far!

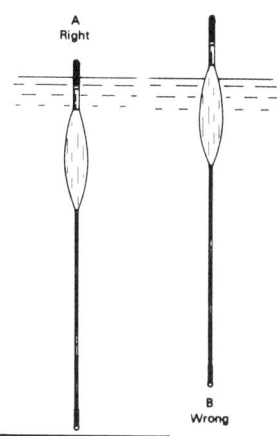

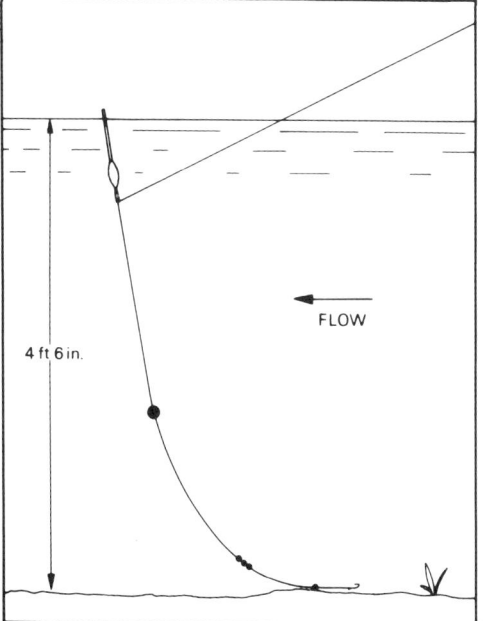

Here is the reverse trotting method as used on the Ant and Thurne and upper section of the tidal Bure. The float is set over-depth and one small shot trails along the bottom. The dragging action of the trail on the bottom induces the float to precede the hook downstream with the flow. The great advantage is that of the bait travels at reduced speed, giving bream more time to make up their minds. The float itself should stand rather more above the surface than is otherwise sensible to provide the necessary buoyancy which allows the trailing bait to lift over mini-obstructions without the float being dragged beneath the surface.

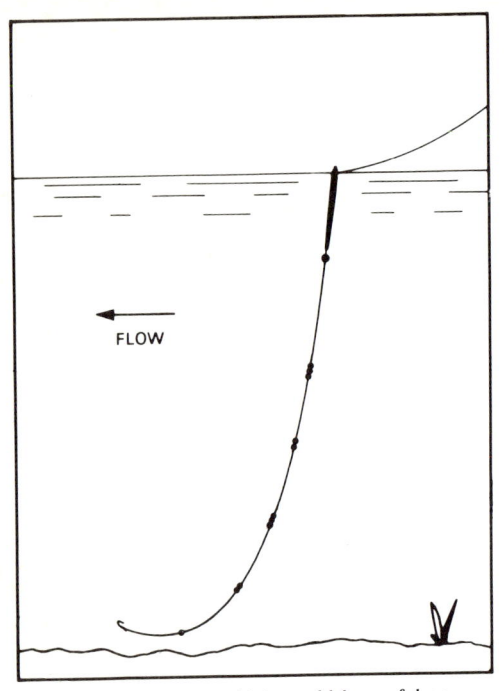

This is a shot pattern which would be useful on the Upper Waveney, Upper Bure or the Wensum. It is used to fish flowing water. The float shown is all-balsa and the shot immediately beneath it helps cock it after the cast. The lower shot are distributed evenly along the distance between float and hook, helping ensure that bait presentation is perfect. The biggest shot is a BB and the remainder are graduated down to a No.8 shot 15 inches from the hook. The number and size of shot in each position is reduced when smaller floats of the same type are used.

10 If you can't catch fish and someone else is doing very nicely, watch and ask how it's done.
11 If you are legering never use a bigger weight than is really necessary to cast the necessary distance and to hold the bait on the bottom. Excepting where the river is flowing strongly, an Arlesey bomb of 3/8oz is ideal.
12 Remember that a leger weight should never be fixed on to the reel line. It should be attached via an 8in long dropper. This allows the fish to move the bite indicator without feeling resistance from the weight.

13 If it proves difficult to catch fish when you feel you are doing everything right it could be that you are fishing at the wrong time. Broadland fishing is best early in the morning and late in the evening throughout the summer.

River Bure

From the angler's point of view at least, the Bure is the most important of the Broads rivers. It rises at Melton Constable and thereafter can be divided into four sections. The first of these, the headwaters, are of no importance in angling terms. It is only immediately above Aylsham that the river contains stocks of coarse fish.

From Aylsham to Horstead mill there is a generally narrow, slow-flowing, clear-water length which is usually excessively weeded in summer. This section is not so well stocked now as it used to be and it seems to me that a fishery management operation could do much to rectify this situation.

There is no boat traffic through the entire length and bank access is limited but past form suggests it is capable of producing quantities of really big fish along the whole section. Among the specimens caught from it are roach to 3lb 7oz, bream to 10lb, dace to just over 1lb and many pike, although these rarely top the 20lb mark.

The clarity of the water allied to the weed growth and lack of pace in the flow makes fish difficult to catch – but this is often the case in waters where quality rather than quantity is the rule. So the most productive fishing times come early and late in the day and after heavy rain. Autumn and winter fishing can often produce the best of the roach sport, particularly when the water is coloured during spells of mild weather.

Anglers are fortunate that much of the length is wide open to fishing, being controlled by the East Suffolk and Norfolk Division of the Anglian Water Authority. The best of the dace are located just above Aylsham but the stock is limited to these fish and roach to Burgh.

Years ago a shoal of big bream was turned into the river at Burgh. These fish showed up spasmodically without ever producing sport of any real quality. It now seems they have died out without leaving progeny behind but this is by no means certain. There has to be a chance of a small number of survivors providing the occasional specimen fish weighing 6lb or more.

The best prospect is in the short length between Burgh Mill and the church, where 2lb roach remain a worthwhile if difficult target.

Anglers who stand on Burgh road bridge and look down into the water will recognize the problems. The water is often so clear that every detail of the riverbed is visible... and this generally means that fishing during the mid-day periods of the summer months can be a complete waste of time.

Night fishing is by far the best. Maggots make a poor bait and most of the big fish are taken on bread paste or flake. Casters can also produce the roach under favourable conditions.

The river bends and winds to Oxnead, where the same stock and fishing conditions exist, but widens just before Buxton Mill. This length for a mile above the mill itself contains some big bream known to weigh as much as 8lb. Individual catches of up to six bream weighing 5lb or more were made near King's Dyke in 1976. Pike are numerous, although a large number were removed by the River Authority as part of a programme intended to give other species a chance to multiply.

Spinning is the most popular method and catches of ten fish a day in the autumn are not unusual. A catch of this proportion can be expected to include at least one double figure fish.

The river has been stocked with various species in what can only be described as a series of haphazard, disjointed efforts. Several hundred chub were put in and have to all intents and purposes disappeared. There is though a chance of getting one or more of these fish from the overflow pool upstream of the mill on the road side of the river.

Below Buxton the fishing is mainly for roach, with some dace and pike. The shoals of bream that used to inhabit the length above Mayton bridge have disappeared.

The river is both narrow and shallow below Mayton bridge, although gaps can be found in the profuse summer weed growth where legered flake can produce big roach and perhaps a bream when the water is tinged with colour.

As the river course winds and twists downstream it reaches extensively wooded and inaccessible areas where big bream are still present. The best fishing, if only because access is available, is above Horstead road bridge. The once-renowned 'Bream Corner', the first bend upstream of the bridge, produces the occasional big bream, as well as roach to 2lb. Tench also show here from time to time.

Below Horstead bridge to the mill there are a number of good swims offering roach and dace. The pike are prolific

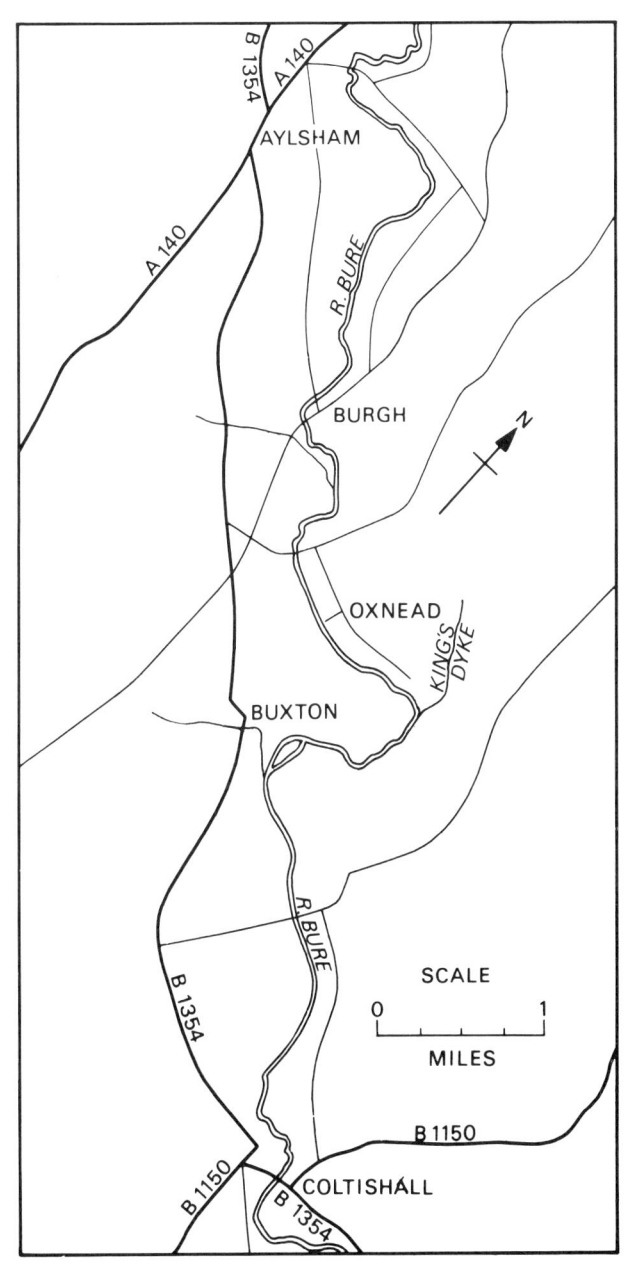

Map 1. River Bure, Aylsham to Coltishall

and if they are generally small they include some bigger fish.

The Bure is navigable just below Horstead Mill but there is little or no access to the river. This is an attractive length, containing some deeper holes beyond the average depth of 4ft with quantities of both big and small bream in residence, as well as roach, dace, tench and pike.

There is free fishing on Coltishall Common but this is a favourite summer mooring point for holiday craft with the result that catches are generally small. This is a far better prospect from autumn onward with some excellent catches of mixed species ranging to beyond 50lb when water conditions are favourable. The deep water at the downstream end of The Anchor Hotel's moorings contains a good head of bream in winter, with the roach concentrated in the area immediately downstream, in the narrow and therefore fast-flowing section.

The Wroxham and District AC has fishing exclusive to its members at Belaugh but this is shallow water constantly pulverized by river traffic during the holiday season.

From Belaugh through to Wroxham there is no worthwhile bank fishing. Swampland behind the river banks makes access impossible. The river is mainly shallow, 4ft to 5ft at normal level, and is little fished. Bream and roach are there to be caught in considerable numbers, with pike and a few tench but the potential has never been exploited. Boats, hired at Wroxham, provide the only means of access.

The river is reed-fringed and attractive along this length and early morning and late evening, as well as fishing after dark, could produce some heavy catches if it was ever given serious attention.

The river both widens and deepens at Wroxham. Again bank access is limited, although some of the boatyards with riverside frontages will allow bank fishing in winter. A ribbon of boat dykes feed into the main river, adding to the water area and, in addition, Bridge Broad and Daisy Broad offer stillwater fishing.

Sport in summer is affected by the river traffic but a number of the boat dykes, paradoxically, are relatively traffic free. They hold considerable stocks of bream, some tench and roach.

The biggest bream catches made in summer come from Bridge Broad, where tench are also numerous, and from the bigger and quieter boat dykes, but the sport in the main river is only of high standard early in the day and after dark.

Holidaymakers staying in waterside bungalows should

groundbait heavily late in the evening and, if they don't fancy fishing through the night, get fishing at first light. This may not give outstanding results first time. Anglers who continue to feed the same swims consistently over a period will eventually be rewarded with heavy catches of bream, with some tench — and the latter could be big fish.

Bream in the tidal Bure from Wroxham to the lower limits are generally up to a 4lb top weight. Small numbers of fish exceed that weight but in the very big catches fish average out at around the $2\frac{1}{2}$ lb mark. Roach are generally quite small — but bigger than they used to be. At one time the Wroxham fishing was bedevilled by massive numbers of tiny roach but fish topping 1lb are now quite common. Bread is the popular after-dark hookbait for bream and this is always likely to bring in roach around or even over the 2lb mark. The tench maximum weight seems a little short of 6lb.

There was a time when Wroxham's perch fishing was of high quality. This is not now so good. The perch disease which swept most of England's coarse fisheries saw them off, but a substantial recovery is under-way and the 2lb-plus fish will soon be showing again in strength. Barring further disease problems, that is.

The Wroxham village area tends to fish rather poorly in late autumn and in the early winter. The water colour created by the boat traffic ends suddenly in later October, the water becomes clear and the bream in particular play hard to get. At such times the boat dykes and broads in the area offer the best prospects, the fish seemingly preferring stillwater when the river is clear.

But heavy rain soon transforms the situation. The water colour that follows gets the bream feeding and sport can be outstanding. I have always found that on days when you can push your fingers beneath the surface and water colour prevents you seeing your finger nails conditions are ideal!

Wroxham hasn't produced hefty bream catches in recent winters and some local anglers take the view that the fish are now not so numerous as they were. I don't agree. Given the right fishing conditions there can be some exceptional sport at Wroxham. The roach too will often show up well in winter when the bigger fish give a better impression. And, all against the calendar, tench are taken with surprising regularity from the area immediately downstream of Wroxham bridge.

The pike fishing is outstanding in winter. In that respect there has been a great improvement. In the period immediately after the Second World War, when I fished the area extensively for pike, I would have said there were

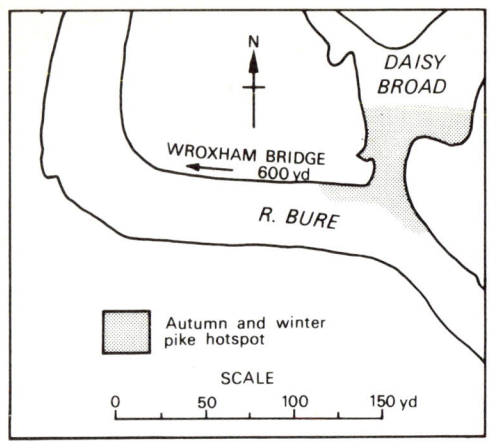

The most productive hotspot for 20lb plus pike in the whole of the Broads area is shown in the shaded section marking the junction of Daisy Broad with the River Bure at Wroxham. The contour of the river takes the flow along the far bank, leaving relatively slack water in and close to the entrance. Fishing from November through the season's end with livebait fished within a foot of the bottom catches most of the pike.

no 20lb pike at all within the village area. Certainly none was ever caught, and of several hundred I took myself the biggest scaled only 17½ lb. Bridge Broad could then produce pike weighing a pound or so more but 20-pounders at least seemed non-existent.

A remarkable change occurred in the early 1970s. Suddenly the pike were bigger and in the years that have followed Wroxham has produced more 20lb fish than any other area of Broadland. The main hotspots have been in the length from the viaduct, above the road bridge and, including Bridge and Daisy Broads, extending to within half a mile of the upstream entrance to Wroxham Broad. There are no complete records of the number of 20-pounders taken but within the last four years the total must be around forty and could be higher. The biggest fish have been 26-pounders and I have the feeling 30-pounders could show by 1980. We shall see!

Although it is now around 25 years since I pike-fished the Wroxham area the pike continue to show in the same areas that produced the biggest fish that long ago. The best section remains the area downstream of Jack Powles' boatyard for some 1000 yards, with the area around and inside and entrance to Daisy Broad the best spot of all.

Bridge Broad holds a good head of pike and a number of 20lb fish are caught there each winter. Bream are also taken from this broad in mid-winter. The broad is private but boats can be hired to fish it.

Livebaiting has always been the best method for big pike here, with spinning producing plenty of fish but mainly small ones.

The winter of 1953 gave me my biggest-ever roach at Wroxham. The 2lb 12oz fish came on bread paste in a catch that included many big bream. That catch coincided with exceptionally strong flood tides ... and the water was heavily coloured.

At one time rudd also showed up regularly in winter. Fish to over 2lb were quite common and I believe there are still enough of these fish living in the back dykes in summer to give some surprising winter sport when they move out into the main water.

At a time when much of the broads area is silting rapidly, the Wroxham area has maintained its depth better than most. This is probably because the riverbanks are piled, with the result that the banks have not been washed away by the wave action created by motorized boat traffic. Certainly it remains an attractive proposition in winter, at times when fish are extremely difficult to contact either upstream or below the village area.

In support of this theory, the lower village limits to Wroxham Broad fish less spectacularly in winter. Bank access is not available through the whole of this length, other than by courtesey of riverside property owners but all types of fishing boats, from those with powered inboard engines to the humble rowing boat, can be hired at Wroxham throughout the fishing season.

Winter catches of roach and bream are generally made on maggots or caster bait. This is a direct contradiction to summer, when bread paste or flake is the best bet.

The bank is heavily wooded and inaccessible most of the distance to Horning but the fish stock is good. The area between the two entrances to Wroxham Broad can fish well in the summer for bream at a time when the bulk of the river traffic takes the detour through the broad itself. The best section is the 500 yards upstream of the lower entrance, with the much deeper water at this lower entrance particularly popular for heavier-than-average roach.

This can be a good spot to fish at first light in high summer but it becomes untenable once the river traffic gets under-way. Night fishing is certainly productive through this section, but my favourite spot is two bends

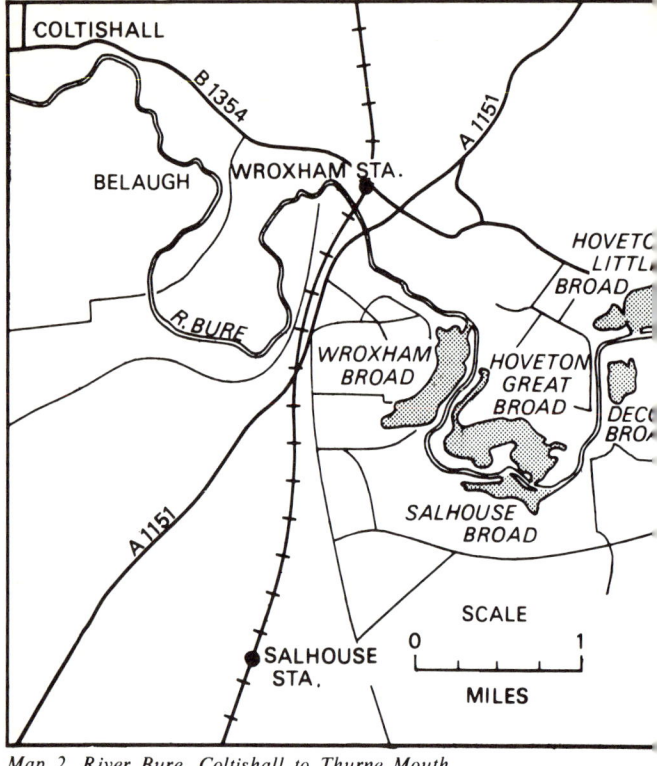

Map 2. River Bure, Coltishall to Thurne Mouth

downstream of the lower entrance. Baiting with bread flake over a heavily groundbaited swim, it is often possible to run up some heavy catches in fast time.

The winter fishing for roach can also be good here, but for some reason best known to themselves the bream do not show so well in winter. Could be that they either move into the broad or travel as far upriver as the village area. The first frosts knock the edge off the fishing here, and although there is some recovery as the cold continues it does not fish as well in the cold weather as the area nearer the village.

Salhouse Little Broad is private. Fishing is not allowed – a pity, because it contains a lot of tench and pike. The bends just upstream of this little broad can fish very well for roach early in the day. Soft processed cheese can be a good bait here. Don't expect to fill a giant keepnet but the few bites are likely to produce roach of 1 ½ lb or better. Cheese, though, is another bait that doesn't do such good work in winter.

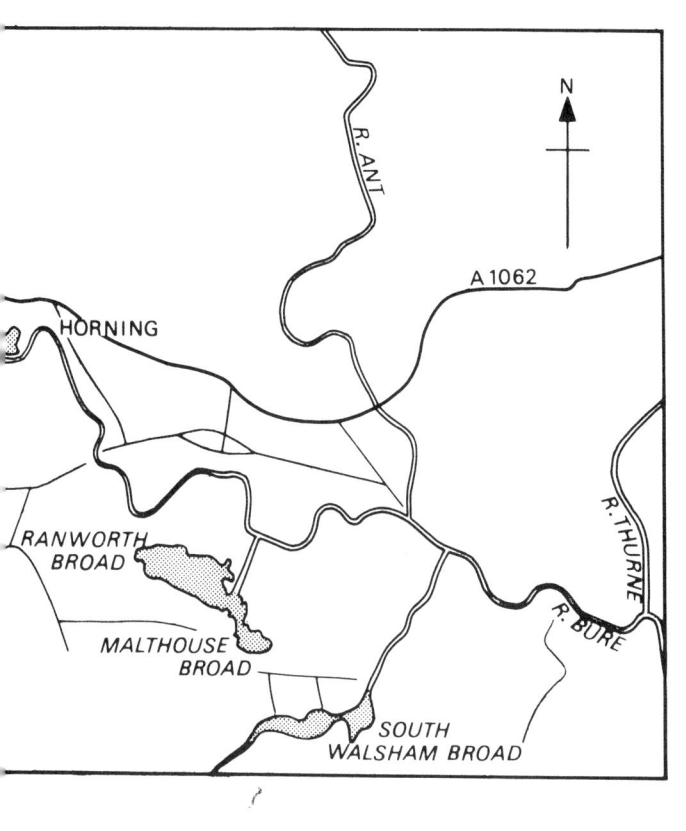

I have never known the section between Salhouse Little Broad and the lower entrance of the bigger Salhouse Broad to fish well. It looks good, maybe it is good, but that has not been my experience so I cannot recommend it.

There is though a substantial improvement below Salhouse towards Woodbastwick. Once again boat fishing is the only way. There's no bank access, but the winter roach can be good, with bream showing from time to time under favourable conditions. The area is well within range of inboard and outboard motor powered fishing boats hired at Horning and Wroxham.

The tidal influence becomes increasingly apparent as we travel downriver. Above Wroxham the flood tide usually means little more than the water's downstream movement either slowing or stopping. At Wroxham the tide moves in both directions, but with the flood tide generally light. Below the big broads at Wroxham, Salhouse, and Hoveton the strength of the tide increases. It is never strong this far upriver but both the ebb and flood present perfect float fishing opportunities with a moving bait.

Hoveton Great Broad is private and is dammed so that there is no access from the main river. The water though shows a marked reluctance to be contained in this way and breaches occur regularly under tidal pressure. Hoveton Broad (and Hudson Bay, which is linked to the broad itself) contains very substantial stocks of pike and bream.

The increased pace of the Bure below Salhouse Broad helps make it ideal roach water and the stock is of mixed sizes but including a higher proportion of fish weighing 1lb and more. The bream are also numerous in all size ranges.

The first major point of access to the river is at Woodbastwick Staithe, a mile below Salhouse Broad. The Norwich and District AA hires the bank fishing on the Woodbastwick side but this is available to members only. A Norwich Association yearly membership book costs £1.50. The association secretary is Cliff Braithwaite, 4, Cranage Road, Lakenham, Norwich (telephone Norwich 25682).

This length of bank has adequate space for 40 anglers at any one time and is used annually for contests after October in which top weights exceed 20lb. Early and late fishing sessions in summer can lead to very big bream catches of 50 – 60lb over heavily-baited swims.

As the river takes a right turn at Didler's Mill a long reach with only modest bends extends through to Horning. This is one of the best areas in the Bure for sustained catches of roach and bream. Pike are also numerous.

Hoveton Little Broad, also known as Black Horse Broad, joins the river on the left. This is a large but private water which is open to navigation throughout the summer season but is closed in winter. At one time it was closed totally but pressure by the boatowners, who had wanted it opened up completely, led to this compromise arrangement.

The real issue here, as with other broads that remain closed, is the definition of tidal water. Costly legal battles have always been avoided by the two factions but if it could be proved conclusively that all or any of the private broads are fully tidal then it seems they would have to be opened.

Riverside bungalows make their first appearance immediately below the point where Hoveton Little Broad joins the Bure. These extend all the way to the Swan Hotel at Horning. The presence of numerous boat dykes, some of them long, wide and quite deep in places, ensures excellent breeding conditions for fish of all species. The dykes contain many tench and pike, some rudd and lots of bream.

Although the broads rivers have silted appreciably as the result of long term bank erosion, the water deepens at Horning to as much as 9ft at normal level. The Swan bend and the area upstream is generously stocked with bream and, despite the heavy summer boat traffic, it is possible to catch fish through the day in favoured areas where the depth provides some immunity for the fish.

The Swan bend itself, an excellent winter hotspot, is much too traffic-laden to remain tenable throughout the day, and at weekends the sailing club, with its headquarters adjacent to the Swan Hotel, adds to the activity. Better to fish in the area beginning 200 yards upstream of the bend.

This area can produce some big pike. These appear to move out of the back dykes in the autumn and specimens up to 26lb are taken each year. Apart from the boat moorings close at the upstream end of the village — and these are, of course, monopolized by boats in the summer — there is no bank access.

That's not to say that individuals cannot obtain permission to fish from some of the privately-owned sections. I have always found it worth asking the question but, of course, permission to fish should never be taken for granted.

The Horning village reach, extending from The Swan to The Ferry, approximately a mile of river, offers excellent fishing throughout. Heavy aggregate catches of bream can be made here by both early morning and night fishing in summer but for pure pleasure and a minimum of disturbance late autumn and winter is really best.

I have always taken the view that any broads holiday of mine would be centred on this area if I were concerned solely for roach and bream fishing. The fishing is consistent, with roach weighing to well over 2lb. At least one fish of over 3lb is on record from this area and the bream, although containing many small fish, include large numbers over the $2\frac{1}{2}$lb mark.

One area much favoured by local and Norwich anglers is the bend upstream of The Ferry. Boats moored across the flow on the inside of the bend (Horning side of the river) obtain huge bream hauls with 60lb a time well within the capacity of the area. Float legering allows boat anglers to fish on bait anchored to the bottom and this is a popular method, but anglers fortunate enough to be able to fish from the shore do very well legering with the quivertip style.

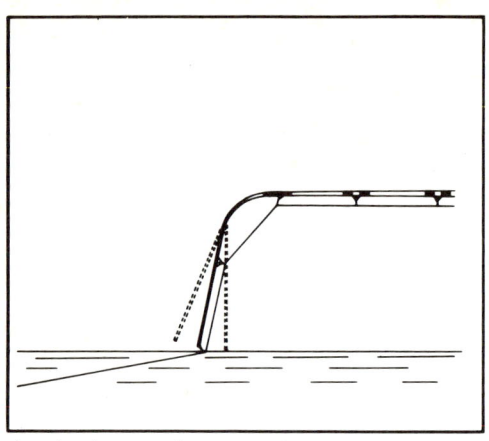

A swingtip correctly positioned to register bites. The extreme end of the tip just touches the water – only touches, doesn't project into it. When a slight bite registers the tip moves clear of the water. A movement of an eighth of an inch is easier to spot in this position than in any other. The tip is marginally extended by a near-taut line. If a fish takes the bait and moves towards the rod the line becomes slack and the swingtip drops backwards to hang vertically. Ideally the rod should be held in three rod rests to keep it steady.

Tench show in the main river from time to time. Back dykes and boat basins off the main river add variety to the geography, creating fish-holding and feeding grounds and adding to the fertility of this section. In winter, particularly during periods when cold, clear water predominates, the bream seem to transfer to the basins from the main river. It is here that very heavy catches are made in often adverse conditions.

Immediately below Horning Ferry on the Woodbastwick side is a long length of bank leased by the East Suffolk and Norfolk Division of the Anglian Water Authority. The access point is immediately opposite The Ferry Inn. This yields some exceptional roach catches. I have seen some as high as 70lb made in a single session on caster bait. Bream are also prolific here with the biggest weights recorded coming halfway along the length at the point where bungalow development on the far bank ends.

The river continues to widen and comes under increasing tidal influence below Horning but quality fishing continues along the entire length to Ant mouth. It is a great shame there is no bank access to this area for it would produce outstanding catches winter and summer alike.

The Bure, and its tributaries Ant and Thurne, suffer from salt tides. Under the worst conditions – after a period of little or no rain combined with strong north-west winds – the strongest tides are increased in strength with the result that sea water pours into the river at Great Yarmouth and forces its way upriver to the lower and even middle sections of Horning.

The fish flee before the encroaching salt with some but usually minimal losses in the Bure. Massive quantities of fish are on the move at such times and the Horning area becomes densely populated and provides remarkable fishing for a time until the fish again move away downstream as the salt water recedes. The periods around new and full moon give the strongest tides and it is then that this phenomena is most likely to occur.

There is bank fishing as far as Ant mouth but on the downstream side Norwich and District AA have the fishing and this is available on a $12\frac{1}{2}$ pence day ticket basis – permits from Ludham Post Office, and at the cottage situated at the top of the access lane. Access is difficult in winter when the fishing can be poor but early morning sport in summer can be good for both roach and bream. At this point the river is subject to strong tidal flow in both directions and although experienced anglers can float fish most successfully those of only modest experience and ability would do better to leger using a quivertip for bite indication.

This section used to be deeper than it is now. Silt has filled the holes formerly used by the bream and catches are not so high as they used to be, but summer fishing can be good through to Thurne Mouth and beyond.

South Walsham Dyke joins the Bure almost opposite the ruins of St Benet's Abbey. The dyke is narrow and shallow but there is some access to the section nearest the broad via South Walsham. Bream can be taken here when boat traffic is light.

Below Thurne Mouth the Bure continues to provide good bream fishing but legering becomes increasingly necessary as the flow increases. One problem here is that the strength of flow sweeps suspended vegetation and debris along at some speed and this can be a continued nuisance when legering.

The best way to minimize the problem is to fish with a long 'tail' between the leger weight and the hook. This can be as much as 4ft and some anglers fish an even longer tail.

The area around Upton, on the Norwich side of the

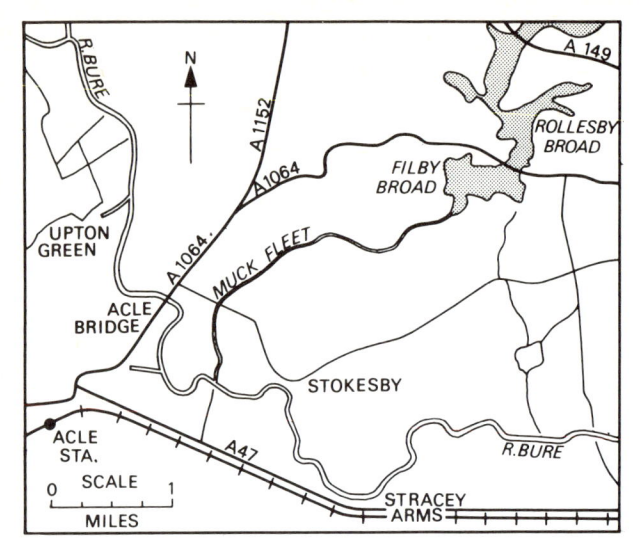

Map 3. River Bure, Thurne Mouth to Stracey Arms

river, is excellent bream fishing in the summer. The best section is downstream of Upton Dyke and halfway to Acle. This means a longish walk but the quality of the fishing makes it worthwhile.

Many of the best catches in this area are made on bread flake, with maggots also more than useful. Worms have never been a popular bait with the local anglers but that's not to say they cannot entice bream at times when other baits fail. Snag is, of course, that eels can then become a nuisance.

The Upton bank and the area around Acle is freely accessible and this happy state continues through the remainder of the river, although this lower section is of decreasing value for a number of reasons. The tide flow becomes very heavy. Salt water infiltration can lead to a situation where there are no fish in residence and the fish stock at best is somewhat migratory.

That's not to say that roach and bream cannot be caught here. They can, of course, and hefty catches are possible to Stokesby and the Stracey Arms. Take the sensible precaution though of tasting the water. If it tastes unduly brackish then don't bother to fish since sport is likely to be slow or non-existent.

The fish in this lower length appear, however, to have developed relative immunity to the salt. They may not like it but circumstances have enabled some of them at least to live with it. During the summer of 1976 the prolonged drought created the conditions for maximum salt penetration. With little or no backwater then coming downstream, the salt swept up the Bure in great force. It was of such duration that green salt water crabs were found in quantity at Acle. During the peak of this salt penetration an angler sat fishing in splendid oblivion, unaware of the situation. A local angler asked him how sport was going only to receive an unexpected answer. The angler had caught seven roach. The fish were roach but the salt had bleached the colour from their body and scales. They were obviously fit and well enough to feed − or they could not have been caught on rod and line. So, anything can happen in fishing. Surprising results − good and bad − occur all the time.

To generalize, though, the Bure is a well stocked river. Its middle reaches are the best. Horning is without question the best angling centre but limited access to the bank remains the biggest problem.

River Ant

The River Ant, which gets its name from its source, Antingham Ponds, is of little value as a fishery in its upper reaches. Although the course of the river from North Walsham downriver to Dilham was canalized in 1832, under the North Walsham and Dilham Canal Company, the canal is now derelict, with most of its locks in ruins and with very little water remaining. Years ago this canal carried wherries loaded with grain and other cargoes, but when the need for the canal waned so the waterway fell into disrepair.

At best the canal is now little more than a drain, for there is no fishing of any note upstream of Honing. Even this modest water suffered heavily from pollution at one time, but major improvements have at least seen the water reach a better standard of purity. Some fish have recently been released in the section above Briggate Lock.

There are strong feelings, notably by the boating fraternity, that the whole of the canal should be restored to navigation. It seems doubtful to me if this will ever be much more than a pipe-dream, but if it were ever done it would recreate many miles of fishing – if slowly. The cost is, of course, the prohibitive factor and it seems that while people are prepared to spend many hours talking about the project, no one is prepared to spend money! Until that day comes anglers need not concern themselves with the Ant above Honing.

The first worthwhile fishing is found below Honing Lock. The water is still very shallow, but it does hold a fine stock of fish. They can come upstream from the lower Ant into this section for Honing's is the last of the locks. There are good numbers of bream here and E. Howard of Worstead took a roach of 3lb 2½oz from it in the early 1950s. It is doubtful if such fish are there at present but the fishing for roach is now improving again following the bad year of 1967-68 when a large proportion of the area's stock died.

Technically this length of water is open for navigation, but very few boats can get so far upriver due to the shallows and the narrowness of the stream, which makes it difficult for the larger motor cruisers to turn around for the return trip to deeper water.

There are plenty of bream all along this length and good aggregate catches can be made. It is not extensively fished and is well worth a visit, particularly in winter. Worm is a good bait for the bream. Access is across Honing Common – anglers should keep to the right when crossing the common, for the marshes to the left are private and fishing is not allowed from them.

Below Honing Common there is little or no public access to the river, which continues to hold a fine head of bream. Below Tonnage Bridge, just over a mile above Wayford Bridge, the river deepens and widens and the lower reaches of this length can be fished by anglers walking upriver from Wayford. There is a little more than 3ft of water at normal level, but there is rarely any degree of flow and it pays to use fine tackle, except at night.

Three hundred yards above Wayford Bridge the canalized section of the Ant ends at the point where it is joined by Dilham Cut. This dyke was dredged seven years ago and this has led to an improvement in its fishing. Bream up to 4lb are found on it, together with some roach and tench, plus the inevitable pike.

Even below Wayford Bridge there is little flow on the river – except after heavy rain. There are large numbers of

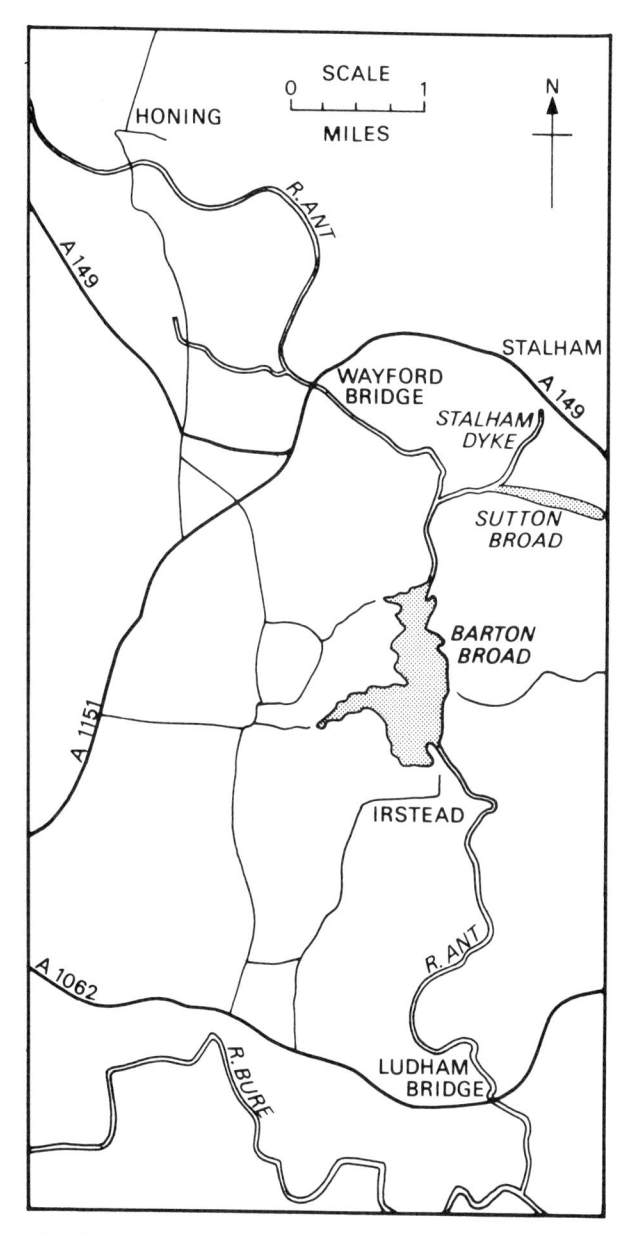

Map 4. River Ant, Honing to Ludham Bridge

bream all along this length and occasionally bream running close the 6lb mark have been taken. There are also good numbers of tench, although these fish are not often caught in any quantity. One noted bream swim is where the sewage outfall from Stalham runs in between Wayford and Hunset Mill. Although they do not run to any great size, there are plenty of pike here and there is good fun to be had with light spinning tackle.

Downstream of Hunset Mill the river banks are heavily fringed with reeds and, as is the case in much of the Ant, where these reeds exist there are always bream. Very often it is not possible to contact the bigger fish, but heavy aggregate catches can be made and this is most enjoyable for anglers who are content with continuous sport rather than big fish. In summer the water tends to be very clear and this can be something of a handicap, particularly when boat traffic is of any strength.

Half a mile below Hunset Mill the main stream is joined by Stalham Dyke. This, too, is generally clear water and the best results are made early and late in the day. Anglers prepared to fish through the night can do very well with the better-quality bream.

Midway along its length to Stalham the dyke is joined by another dyke leading to Sutton staithe. What used to be Sutton Broad is found above the junction. Years ago it was an extensive piece of water but it has silted considerably and the only open water remaining is the navigable channel through the middle.

As happened on many of the overgrown and silted waters, the coypu, when it was in its heyday five years ago, made great inroads into the vegetation. This outsized rodent of South American origin, which escaped to the area from farms where it was bred for its skin, subsequently multiplied alarmingly. Not only were its numbers decimated by the cold of severe winters but an intensive anti-coypu campaign followed, once it had been classified a pest. However, though coypu cannot now be seen so frequently as a few years back, it has a remarkable capacity to increase in number and, despite everything that can be done to keep numbers down, it is now with us permanently.

Excellent bream catches are made in the boat basins at Stalham, although the fish tend to be of only modest size. There is no bank fishing in the Ant from Stalham Dyke down to Barton Broad, where the river merges with the wide expanse of water, running along its length to emerge at Irstead.

The first reaches of the Ant below Barton Broad, those

closest to Irstead, used to be crammed with small bream. Unfortunately the Ant is not now the prolific fishery it was 15 years ago and the stock has thinned appreciably.

The first reach out of Barton Broad is much wider than the section immediately after. This makes it a better proposition for day time fishing in the summer when boat traffic is at peak strength. The catches there are mainly roach and bream, the former stopping at 1lb whereas the bream run to over 3lb. The best of the bream fishing is at night, although daylight fishing in the autumn can produce better catches than are made in high summer.

The next section to Irstead staithe is very narrow. Big cruisers have some difficulty passing — and the additional complication of an angler fishing from a boat here can lead to problems! It was here that John Bullock, of Bedford, won the 1967 Norfolk Broads Championship, a contest fished annually in October, with a match record weight of 65lb. A number of other catches made in the same area topped 40lb in one of the most dramatic weigh-ins match angling can have known.

Bream are still resident in this area but autumn and winter fishing now produce the best results. The area can fish badly for weeks on end and then suddenly and quite out of the blue the fishing re-establishes itself at a high level before deteriorating again.

There are some pike in this area but the roach are small and not numerous. Irstead used to be a grand spot for big perch and if this too is no longer as good a prospect as it was there has to be a chance of its recovery when the perch population increases after the disease.

The quality of the fishing is varied through the next length, extending downsteam to How Hill. This area was once a remarkable bream length and some extremely heavy match weights have been taken there. The last National Championship to be fished in the Broads area, taking in the Ant, the Bure from above Ant mouth to beyond Acle and the Thurne below Potter Heigham, was won here by David Groom of Leighton Buzzard with a weight of 37lb. Local opinion is that it is extremely doubtful if the National Championship can ever again be fished in Broadland.

The high level of boat traffic through the autumn — and this has increased dramatically in the last ten years — makes the area an unacceptable venue for many of the competitors. How Hill fishing costs 20 pence a day. The bailiff collects.

From here to Ant mouth there are no pike or tench worth mention. It would be a major surprise if anyone caught one fish of either species — although the cocky ruffes are large and an Ant fish once came within 6dr of the national record of 3oz 12dr.

It is perhaps the greatest single tragedy from a bank fishing viewpoint that the Ant from How Hill to the Bure has deteriorated so much. Immediately after the Second World War big catches of bream and roach — with tench and pike — could be taken all along but it is now rated barely worth fishing. Local anglers avoid it since it is so narrow and shallow and enjoyable fishing is never possible in mid-summer simply because of the never-ending boat traffic.

The boats have, in fact, driven the fish out. There is no shelter for them, no weed growth, no width, no escape, so, excepting for smaller fish, mainly immature roach, the stock has gone.

From time to time though the unexpected happens. In the summer of 1976 the continuous salt tides, which reached further up the Ant than usual, pushed hordes of lower Bure bream into the river. These fish showed mainly in the Johnson Street to Irstead section and some heavy catches were made for a time. The snag is, of course, that these fish only stay long enough for the Bure to empty of salt before departing to their former homes.

Sometimes roach and small bream can be taken either side of Ludham Bridge in mid-winter. Assumedly they leave the Bure and take up residence in this area but the fishing is so unpredictable that it really isn't worth taking seriously.

There is bank fishing available along the whole length of the Ant on one bank or the other from How Hill to the Bure — and there are very few fish to make it worth using. On occasions bream and some roach can be taken in the last 150 yards where the Ant joins the Bure but this is unpredictable fishing, the narrow river having little to offer either the fish or the angler with the counter-attractions of the Bure so close.

The Ant then is a rather poor prospect. The best fishing in its area has to be Barton Broad itself and the river closest to the broad. As I see it, the river has little prospect of making any return to form unless it is deepened. A programme of dredging from Barton to the Bure, to add 2ft of depth, is needed if the fish are to find the river habitable.

It is tidal from Barton to the Bure with a strong flow in both directions, although the ebb usually carries most pace. It is not an ideal river to leger and float fishing brings the best returns. When the wind is blowing in the opposite direction to the flow there are ideal fishing conditions. The speed of the float's travel down-tide is slowed by the wind and this creates the best conditions for taking bream.

It pays to fish marginally over-depth since this too slows the bait's movement in the tide and gives the slow-feeding bream a little more time in which to make up their minds about feeding as the bait moves past.

Some of the most productive areas always used to be where the angler cast towards a reed bed. It could be that the tall reeds help maintain a less disturbed patch of water since the motor cruisers seldom pass as close to the bank as they would were the shoreline more open.

Night fishing above and below Barton Broad can produce 50lb catches or better, with bread flake and paste getting top marks as bait. During the day maggots become a better prospect, in a swim either loose-fed with maggots or given a little-but-often groundbait-and-maggots treatment.

River Thurne

The Thurne is only five miles long but enjoys a reputation out of all proportion to its length. The most favourable aspect about it is that from its beginning at Somerton, close to the coast road, to its junction witn the Bure at Thurnemouth there is widespread access to the bank.

Much of the bank is owned by the Anglian Water Authority and the only substantial length not otherwise available is the Thurne Mouth to Womack Dyke section on the Ludham side. This is controlled by the Norwich and District AA and $12\frac{1}{2}$ pence day tickets are available in Ludham. Long stretches each side of Potter Heigham, extending from Martham to Repps, are fronted by holiday chalets and boatyards and many of these can be fished from on application.

The Thurne has had a chequered career. It carried a massive fish population immediately after the Second World War but successive salt tides diminished the stock. At times the area each side of Potter Heigham bridge was carpeted with dead bream and roach but the river's near-incredible capacity to survive as a fishery saw it through the many crises. Many of the fish were always able to flee upstream to Heigham Sound and beyond Martham, returning when the salt receded.

No matter what the losses in the river, the existence of mammoth stocks of big bream in the Hickling – Heigham Sound complex was always sufficient quickly to replenish the denuded areas.

The situation changed drastically in 1969 when a

39

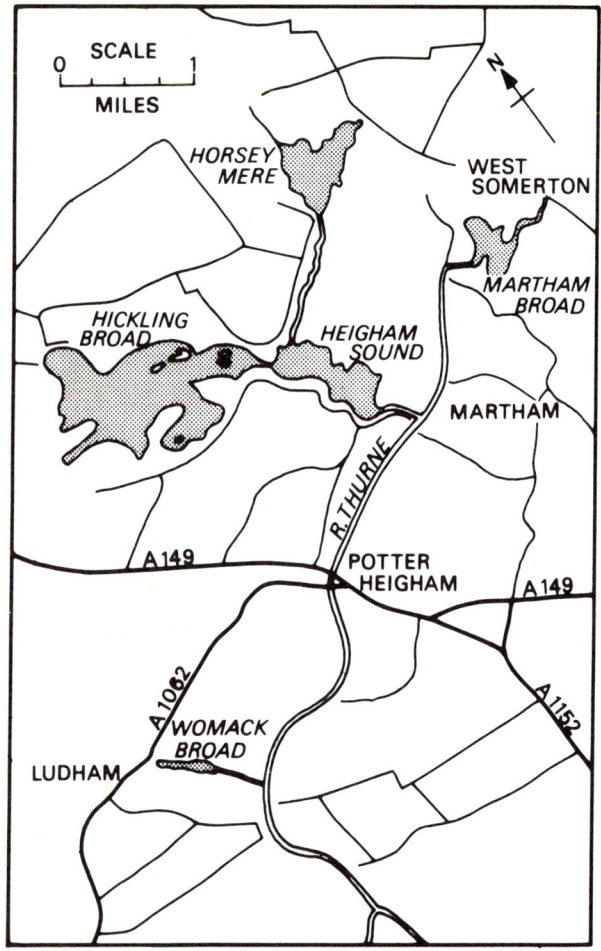

Map 5. River Thurne, Hickling Broad, Heigham Sound and Horsey Mere

prymnesium outbreak devastated the stocks in these upper waters, including Martham and Somerton Broads. Prymnesium is an algal organism which becomes toxic when it dies, denuding the water of oxygen and killing all species of fish, eels included.

No one will ever know the proportion or tonnage of the fish killed but despite staggering losses, put by one authority at 200 tons, huge shoals of fish escaped to the Thurne and relative immunity.

Prymnesium is still present in the upper Thurne area and

the count increases dramatically from time to time. There has never again been such a massive fish kill, although the threat remains. But the major losses in the breeding areas combined with the effect of salt tides have limited the Thurne's capacity to maintain its fish stock.

If the river's future to some extent at least remains finely-balanced, there has been a partial recovery and quality catches continue to be made. There tend to be some short understocked stretches while others nearby contain ample fish and since these are never in the same places for long the fishing tends to be patchy. Despite these shortcomings, the river can be expected to show considerable improvement so long as the build up is allowed to continue without further losses. And the stock is by no means modest at this time.

The Thurne is a shallow river. It is rarely deeper than 5ft so it suffers from the massive boat traffic in summer. But fish remain in the river and catches of high aggregate weights are made early in the day and particularly after dark, many of them by anglers holidaying in the riverside bungalows.

As happens when the fish stock of any fishery diminishes, the remaining bream grow rather bigger than they did previously. So Thurne bream to over 5lb can now be caught, whereas the ceiling was little over 4lb years ago. Roach are widespread and many of these are good sizeable fish to 1lb and more.

There is, though, little by way of back-up species. Perch are few, pike remain scarce and there are no tench worth mention. None of this matters too much and so long as the bream and roach are able to provide good sport this is sufficient for most anglers.

Bream catches of over 100lb at a sitting have been made in recent years, with roach weights over 50lb, so there is clearly ample opportunity for some good returns. Sport though is unpredictable. One angler can make a mammoth catch while others fishing nearby are unable to get even so much as a bite.

Different sections put up varied performances winter and summer. The Thurne Mouth to Potter Heigham length generally fishes best in the summer, producing mainly bream. The Repps area, at the lower line of the holiday bungalows, is marginally deeper and is therefore able to provide more consistent fishing, with a bigger proportion of quality fish.

Womack Dyke, which joins the Thurne at the upstream end of the Norwich Association water, contains some roach and bream and there are some pike in the open water at the extreme end. But this dyke has seen massive mortalities during salt tides when fish have become trapped.

The Thurne below Potter Heigham bridge is patchy in winter. The Repps area can be relied on to give the best fishing but the lower section closest to the Bure loses its form as the stock moves away.

When cold weather comes there can be days when the fish, mainly roach then, can only be caught in the very short length between Potter Heigham's two road bridges. Goodness only knows why, but this happens.

The tidal influence is quite strong between Thurne Mouth and Candle Dyke because of the movement of water on and off the 1,000 or so acres of water at the head of the river. This helps provide quality float fishing, although many of the big catches of bream are made legering.

The High's Mill to Candle Dyke patch fishes well, especially in the winter. After strong tides concentrations of bream are found in the area between Martham Ferry and Martham Broad. There can be good catches, though, roach included, in the short stretch between Martham Ferry and Candle Dyke.

The upstream length to Martham Broad is patchy. Some of the better results come in the 400 yards immediately above the ferry and a long walk in the Martham Broad direction is not always rewarded.

Before prymnesium did its worst there used to be a strong head of tench in this length, with Dungeon Corner, the first bend in the long strait above the ferry, the hotspot. Many of these fish used to move in and out of Martham and Somerton Broads, but sad to tell most of them died there when prymnesium was at its peak. I saw large numbers of quality fish both dead on the bottom on the two broads and floating away downstream on the surface.

As yet there has been no substantial improvement in the tench stock but the ground is right for them and given time the situation can be expected to rectify itself — although introductions of middle-weight tench would help speed the process.

The two broads are private. There is every reason to believe their pike population has shown radical improvement since the disaster, although many fish died there at the time.

One of the prymnesium-free zones established itself in the section beyond the two broads to Somerton. Large numbers of fish — tench, pike, bream and roach — found sanctuary here and survived to provide the breeding nucleus to begin the restoration.

Pike of 20lb have been taken in the river here and on the

broads in recent years. The worst could be over and by 1980 the Upper Thurne could be back at its best. Oddly enough there was no sign of dead rudd during the mortality and if this is taken as a happy omen that must be tempered with the thought that few have been caught since. However any river with the fertility of the Thurne must have some chance of a complete recovery.

The length from Somerton downstream to the two broads contains quantities of fish − pike, bream and roach mainly − and the lower section can yield good weights both to early morning fishing in summer, to night sessions and to winter efforts.

Bread is a good summer bait for the bream, which in winter seem to prefer maggots and casters. The roach are happy with casters or maggots, although there are days when they will show a preference for one or the other. Red maggots have become a popular bait on many of the country's open match rivers but Thurne roach showed this preference many years ago and it is always worthwhile including maggots of mixed colours in the preparations for a day's sport. Sometimes the preference is for orange, other days red is best. There are no hard and fast rules by which you can tell in advance which is best. You have to fish it to find out for yourself!

If some passages of my commentary on the affairs of this river make gloomy reading, rest assured there are plenty of fish to be caught.

River Yare

The Yare is a river of two sections: one tidal and navigable, the other having no access for power boats. Norwich is roughly the dividing line between the two sections, with excellent roach and chub fishing dominating the upper half and bream showing in strength through the lower tidal reaches.

The river rises at Shipdham but is of no consequence as a fishery until it has reached Barford, ten miles away. Here the river comes alive. There are roach, dace and pike in the section to Marlingford. Below Marlingford to Bawburgh the river deepens and the roach fishing becomes of top quality. Chub are also present in some strength.

Chub are comparative newcomers to the river. Substantial numbers were turned loose some 15 years ago and they have thrived in quite remarkable fashion. The original fish both packed on weight and spawned successfully, with the result that there are now many times the number of chub that were originally released.

There is some bank access to this area via fisheries leased by the Anglian Water Authority. The length further upstream is on the left bank between Marlingford and Bawburgh, at Easton, and extends for 660 yards.

Below Bawburgh the Anglian Water Authority controls the fishing on one or other bank and sometimes on both all the way downstream to Colney. Immediately below Bawburgh road bridge the Authority has the right bank excluding the area adjacent to Coney Hall but continuing thereafter to Colney itself.

The Authority's left bank holding begins some 500 yards below Bawburgh and this extends for rather more than one mile. This is some of the best water in the Yare. The chub show all the way through and although no one has so far reported an outstanding aggregate weight of these fish local anglers expect to catch two or three when seriously chubbing... and they can weigh up to 5lb and perhaps more.

This Bawburgh downstream section was always one of the best roach waters. Perhaps the arrival of the chub has limited the stock of roach since clearly only a limited number of fish can thrive in any one water and chub are, after all, fry-eaters, but the roach reach an excellent size with 2-pounders taken annually.

The best on record for this stretch weighed 2lb 15oz and the catch that day, made by Tony Emden, included other magnificent roach weighing 2lb 12oz, 2lb 11oz and 2lb 8oz, as well as many others over the 1lb mark. This is comfortable float fishing, with bread the favoured bait for the big fish. Maggots have a tendency to attract the smaller fish.

Grayling were introduced below Bawburgh Mill at the same time as the chub. These fish gave a good account of themselves for a time but although they have reproduced, they have not multiplied in the way the chub have done. One would need to be an optimist to go fishing exclusively for grayling... although anglers may well catch one or more while fishing for other species.

The weed growth can present problems in summer, particularly during periods of drought, and therefore, slow flow. The best fishing comes in late autumn and winter when the weed is knocked down by frost and when the flow rate can be expected to increase substantially. An increased flow will, of course, add colour to the water and this helps the angler to keep the fish feeding.

Below Colney the Authority has all of the right bank to within 300 yards of Earlham bridge. It has another small plot of 100 yards immediately below the bridge, again on the right bank followed by a short break before continuing on downstream for a further 1,500 yards.

The fishing open to all licence holders continues to within 300 yards of Cringleford road bridge. Access to this lower length is at Newfound Farm. On the opposite bank, on the Norwich side of the river, the Authority also has the fishing from Bluebell Road to Cringleford.

This can be difficult water in the summer but no one need doubt the quality of its roach stock — even though it may never again rival its stock of some 15 years ago when anglers caught as much as a hundredweight of roach at a sitting. The roach run to over 2lb. Oddly enough, despite the enormity of the roach population through the years there has never been a 3-pounder fully authenticated.

No one need be unduly surprised if he catches a bream here. These fish are not numerous but small transplants have taken place and the surviving fish are believed to run to 7lb. After-dark fishing in the summer could turn up one of these fish and even a tench or two.

Trout show from time to time through the whole of this upper river. As part of what might at one time have been described as an obsession with these fish, substantial numbers were released into the river. Trout fishing was never ever a serious proposition but the occasional fish weighing up to 6lb is caught by anglers fishing for other species.

The chub and dace are of good quality through the Colney to Cringleford area. Cringleford Mill pool is private but there is free fishing via Church Lane down to the next mill, at Keswick, where the mill pool is private.

From Keswick the river runs through meadowland to pass under the main Norwich to Ipswich road. I haven't fished this area for some years. When I did the roach were of good quality and numerous but it does seem to have deteriorated at least to an extent. That's not to say there are no longer 2-pounders here—there must be, and some sporting dace.

The Yare continues its turn around the outer perimeter of Norwich, through Harford and Old Lakenham to Trowse, where it becomes tidal water below the mill pool. Chub are scattered through this length with 3- and 4-pounders being caught from favoured swims all along.

Roach run big. Two pounders, although never to be described as common, are always a possibility and the fish weigh to $2\frac{1}{2}$ lb. Again this is at its best in autumn and winter.

There are some tench although these are rarely caught. Even rarer now are the big perch and rudd that used to inhabit the length immediately above Trowse Mill.

The mill pool at Trowse is private, but anglers can fish it from a boat. The pool holds quantities of all species but the biggest delight has to be a big shoal of fine chub. Some of those fish weigh in excess of 5lb. There are many roach, some of them big ones, dace, a few pike – with big ones among them – and even a barbel or two.

Barbel were released into the Wensum in two separate batches involving less than 200 fish. Some of these moved downstream into the lower Wensum and from there can reach the tidal Yare.

Don't imagine for one moment this can be described as barbel fishing–but hopefully these fish will multiply with time and could make an impact, if not on the Yare then surely in the Wensum.

The remaining mile of the Yare moves downstream through fields and wooded terrain before merging with the Wensum. At that point the Wensum loses its identity and it is the Yare that flows onward to the sea.

There is some free fishing on the left bank but the Reckitt and Colman land is strictly private. On the opposite bank, where Church Dyke reaches the river, the Norwich and District AA has the fishing rights through almost to the junction with the Wensum. This is day ticket water and is available at 12½ pence per day. The contact is Norwich association secretary Cliff Braithwaite.

Roach fishing can be impressive through this section. I have had a number of fine catches there myself, including one of 42lb. More recently the bream have increased in quantity and size. At one time they were something of a rarity but there are occasions when anglers now catch a bigger weight of bream than roach.

The chub here are concentrated in the mill area upstream but if the species continues to show the same increase apparent over recent years then the lower length to the big river could show good form in the coming years.

Once the upper river merges with the Yare it undergoes a complete change of character. It becomes a wide, deep, fast-flowing river that carries timber, grain and coal boats of up to 500 tons from the sea to Norwich. From this point to the sea it has a minimum width of 30 yards and is often much wider.

These coasters in no way affect the fish stocks. Roach are widespread and in the autumn and winter are easy prey to the angler who sets his stall out for them. Maggots and casters are equally successful, although as in all roach waters caster has the happy knack of producing a consistently better stamp of fish.

Roach of 1lb are common and there is some chance of 2-pounders. This big river also holds a substantial head of bream that don't show as often as the local anglers would like but which nonetheless can provide heavy catches when they are in the right mood.

At one time all the Yare immediately below Norwich suffered from industrial pollution but this situation has been gradually improved over the last 30 years so that there are now no fishless sections in the river. There is the occasional small pollution—nothing is ever perfect—but the fish are numerous enough and the river big enough for there to be no real danger.

This length of the upper tidal river suddenly became transformed when the pollution eased. The fish came apparently from nowhere, emphasizing that provided coarse fish are given clean rivers they are usually more than able to look after themselves. Small numbers of fish can multiply very fast when the environment permits. A restocking policy would rarely achieve the same result and the continuing lesson in that respect is that nature will not be hurried.

Half a mile below the junction of the Wensum and the Yare the main river splits into two. One arm swings off to the left to Thorpe Green, returning to link up again with the river just before Whitlingham. Earlier this century this mile-long arm carried a great head of pike. The fish thinned out but are making a slow return. There is some free and accessible bank fishing, notably at Thorpe Green where there is ample space for 12 anglers. This length can usually be relied upon to provide sport with roach up to 1lb.

These roach run through the entire Thorpe length and there are times, particularly after dark, when the bream can also be caught in fair numbers. These bream are not usually the biggest the Yare has on offer but fish to 3lb show regularly during summer and autumn.

The rate of flow is much less in this backwater than in the main river and it is not as deep. At normal level the main river has an average depth of around 12 ft. It is accessible on both banks in the Whitlingham area, where the fishing is free. Roach are the dominant species. The bream are always a possibility and there's an outside chance of a tench in summer, particularly in the few weeded dykes and in the slack water on the bends in the river.

Norwich anglers take most of their fish in this area on caster and this has done a good job here. On better days, days when the weather and water conditions are right, there's every chance of individual catches approaching 40lb. The autumn has to have the best overall prospects simply

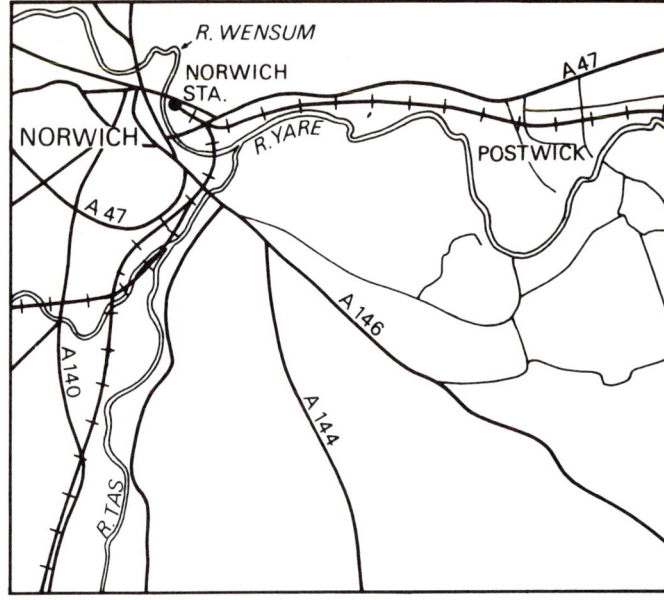

Map 6. River Yare, Norwich to Reedham

because the water is more likely to be coloured. River traffic, though it does exist in summer, is not the hazard here that it is on the Bure, Thurne and Ant because of the additional depth.

There is some bank access to the fishing at Bramerton on the north bank of the river where bream are rather more numerous but the roach continue to show in quantity. On favourable tides it is comfortable float fishing down the middle of the river and big roach catches are made this way and can be expected to include some bream, at least at times.

The biggest of the bream catches though are generally made over heavily baited swims, whereas swim feeding for roach is generally much lighter. When the river is in full flow it usually becomes necessary to leger with a quivertip or to float fish along the margins. Caster will, of course, take the bream, but bread and worm are better baits when bream are sought exclusively.

A mile below Bramerton the Anglian Water Authority has 600 yards of bank fishing on the upstream side of the access point to Surlingham. The remnants of Surlingham Broad are on the southern side of the river between Postwick and Strumpshaw. The water area of this broad is now only a fraction of what it was but roach and bream can be caught there. Anglers should be aware, though, that the water area shrinks fast on an ebb tide and it is possible to become marooned.

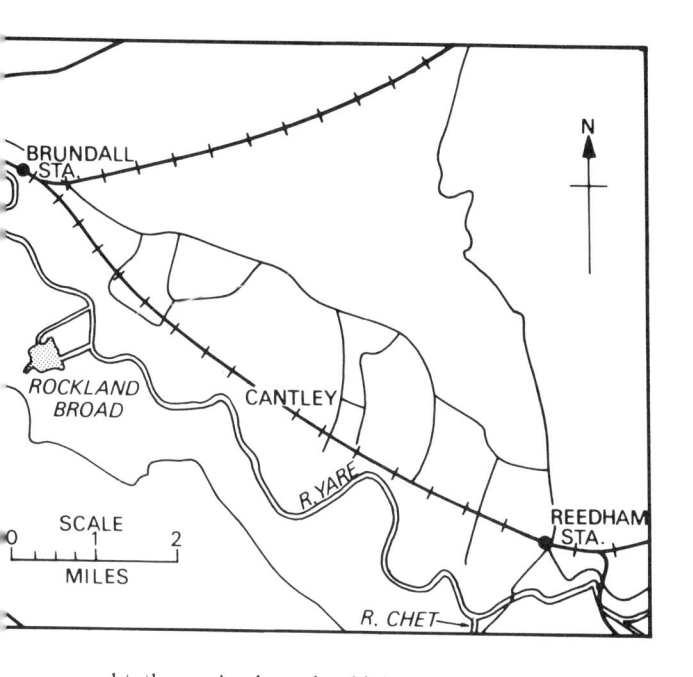

Brundall offers roach and bream, with some sport in the boat dykes. Pike are a serious proposition in the main river as well as in the dykes, although few if any anglers take them seriously. The food-fish stock is so vast that the small pike must grow to big ones, probably very big ones. If the most ardent of pike anglers made a sustained effort, preferably collectively, in this area down in Buckenham they would have a good chance, I think, of fish running close to 30lb.

There is mile after mile of excellent bank fishing and if only the access was better this section of the river would make a perfect venue for a National Championship. Unfortunately it isn't fished to the same extent as the other Broads rivers, with the result that it has never acquired the reputation it really merits.

Access to the river across Strumpshaw marshes is difficult and on the opposite side is the narrow dyke leading to Rockland Broad.

Downstream of Rockland the next point of interest is Buckenham, where the Anglian Water Authority has extensive bank fishing which is available to one and all. Norwich clubs hold contests in this section with great success – although they have to arrange the dates to get the most favourable tide, preferably a flood tide, which is less powerful than the ebb.

It is believed that the Yare's biggest bream concentrations are in this area and swingtipping has brought catches of well over 60lb. One match weight of 60lb has been recorded. Despite the power of the tide the occasional tench can be caught in the shelter of the bends.

The bream fishing really calls for substantial groundbaiting for swim-feeder tactics have paid off for the local anglers and is to be recommended. I have to say this isn't a method of fishing that appeals to me, but it produces good catches.

The Water Authority has 2500 yards on the north bank and on the southern side nearly three miles of bank is available. The southern bank extends from Clacton marshes downstream with the principal access points at the Beauchamp Arms, Langley Green and near Langley Abbey.

The Langley area, as at Buckenham, offers roach and bream, with roach also showing in Langley Dyke. Bream can be taken in this dyke from time to time. The best bream pitches are close to the Yare itself.

The Anglian Water Authority has a short length, 400 yards, on the north bank at Cantley but this is so far downstream we are into a very powerful river. No reservations about the stock-bream and roach are there in some strength, but this far down the river is subject to salt tide encroachment.

There is access to the river at many points but few anglers take this section very seriously. Big bream, fish frequently topping 3lb, are caught here with some quality roach but it is all leger fishing, and with the salt possibility tending to make the fish somewhat migratory there is never any guarantee that the fish will either be present or that they will feed.

Under the right tidal conditions bream and roach can be caught as far as Reedham and even nearer the sea but this section cannot be recommended when there is so much good fishing nearer Norwich, with the guarantee of ample space and limited pressure.

The Yare is a great river in all senses. It may play a bigger part in broads fishing in the next 25 years than it did in the last ... and may prove a more than competent substitute for the traffic-laden Bure, Thurne and Ant.

River Chet

The Chet is a little-known tributary of the Yare, running into the main river at Hardley Cross. It rises at Poringland and has a length of about ten miles. The upper reaches are either of no interest angling-wise or are private and it is only in the three miles of river between Loddon and the Yare that coarse fishing is available.

Roach are the primary species from Loddon downstream. There is considerable access to the left-hand bank, down river past the boatyards. The river is narrow and has a depth of no more than 4ft, although it does deepen just before its junction with the Yare. Many of the roach appear to be small, and although the limited fishing effort is concentrated in the Loddon area there could and most likely must be better fish further downstream. There are points of access to the Chet at Chedgrave.

There are some dace and bream present whenever they decide to move up from their home in the Yare. The best results come in the autumn and winter when the river is quiet, for in recent years the Loddon area has seen extensive boatyard development, leading to more traffic in this narrow waterway.

A mile below Loddon, behind the river wall on the left-hand bank, there are areas of flooded marshland known to hold substantial numbers of pike and many bream. Pike over 20lb have been taken but the fishing is private.

Boats can be hired at Loddon during the normal boating season but winter prospects of obtaining a boat are less favourable.

River Tas

Through most of its sixteen miles the Tas is an attractive little river but regrettably the fishing is private over almost all of its length. It has a good stock of trout in most sections—which explains why there is no place for the coarse fisherman.

If the coarse fishermen are excluded it has proved impossible to exclude the coarse fish. There are some very good roach, some really outstanding dace, a few pike and a small number of grayling.

Records show that at least two dace of 1lb 1oz or better have been taken from the Tas but the best roach fishing that it in any way available is in the Arminghall area. Roach to 2lb 8oz have been taken there and there are a healthy number of 2-pounders available to the few anglers who are able to cast a line for them.

The Tas rises just south of New Buckenham and by the time it reaches Forncett is big enough to contain coarse fish—most of them dace. The river flows through Hampton and Tasburgh before widening considerably on the upstream side of Newton Flotman mill. Below the mill the river is narrower for a time but there are good roach along most of it.

Water levels are low at Shotesham but dace and some trout can be taken from what was once the mill pool. From Newton Flotman, through Stoke Holy Cross and Dunston the river is in the hands of trout syndicates, with no access for the coarse fisherman.

Below Arminghall the river runs close to the Yare. There are some stretches here that can be fished, notably on the right-hand bank where the roach fishing for big fish is very worthwhile. The Tas joins the Yare 400 yards above Trowse Mill.

The sidestream which used to flow down past Trowse Church to link with the Yare 200 yards from the church has been blocked off so that water no longer flows through it from the upper river. Which is a pity. It has become extensively weeded and the shoals of quality dace that used to live in it have disappeared.

River Waveney

The Waveney makes a major contribution to the wealth of fishing in Broadland. The river marks the country border between Norfolk and Suffolk over its entire course but is linked to only one broad, that at Oulton.

The Waveney rises in fen country two miles west of Diss but is of no account as a fishery until it has passed under the main Norwich to Ipswich road at Scole, a mile east of Diss. It is very shallow and heavily weeded in summer but this is the beginning of a river held especially dear by those who love the finer points of roach fishing.

Roach are the primary species in the upper river, with bream becoming much more numerous in the tidal lower section commencing at Ellingham. There is though another ingredient into the sporting potential of the river... chub. These were first introduced into the river some 20 years ago and although they were received with mixed feelings there is no doubt that this is one stocking with a hitherto absent species which has paid off. The chub have multiplied and grown. Some are so big that there is every chance of the Waveney one day providing a fish to take the British

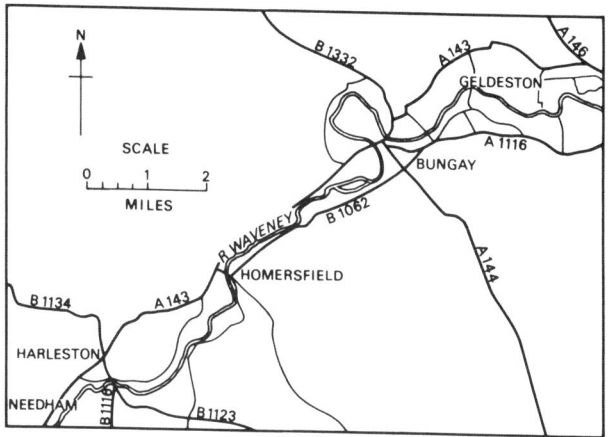

Map 7. River Waveney, Needham to Geldeston

record. Five-pounders are relatively common and the small fish which will provide tomorrow's sport are numerous. It is particularly pleasing that the coming of the chub has in no way diminished the river's roach population and the Waveney continues to produce specimen roach every season.

The upper section in the Scole area is good for little except dace, some roach and small pike but the river takes on additional strength on the way to Hoxne as sidestreams join the main river. One of these, the River Dove, is not without significance of its own. It contains some quality dace topping 12oz and 2lb roach are taken from it from time to time.

The deepening and widening river below Hoxne contains more roach, dace and pike, with the first tench and some trout. The river winds and bends its way downstream providing swims up to 4ft deep with some deeper areas on the bends.

There are no bream this far up the river and the chub are also found lower down but the roach stock is excellent if not always easy to tempt. The water tends to be clear and well-weeded in summer and the best results are made from autumn onward into winter when the weed has disappeared, the flow rate increased and when the water is usually not quite so clear.

Fishing rights in this upper section are in the hands of the farmer riparian owners who must be approached for permission to fish. The Anglian Water Authority leases a number of stretches on the river but none of these is in this upper section.

The area through Syleham and Brockdish is mainly quality roach fishing where the catches are rarely exceptional in their total weight but where the quality of the fish is high. Pound roach are numerous and 2-pounders are there to be caught.

Between Brockdish and Needham is the first Water-Authority-controlled fishing bank. It is reached from Mill Lane which branches off the Diss to Harleston road. Beyond the lane there is a footpath which leads to the 500-yard long stretch.

The river above Needham mill was dredged in 1965 so this area is deeper than other nearby sections and it contains quality roach. Wheat and bread baits are very effective here, with casters also a good bait for the quality fish. There is another stretch of Water Authority bank on the left-hand bank, looking downstream, below Needham Mill.

The Harleston, Wortwell and District Angling Club has the bank at intervals from Needham down to Mendham on the Norfolk side of the river. There are no day tickets available but visitors can join the club as full members for £2.50 and can then fish the club bank. The secretary is J. Adamson, 21 Thomas Manning Road, Diss, Norfolk.

The club also controls the fishing in Weybread Pits. These have a total water area of approximately 40 acres and contain a very mixed fish population. There are big carp and pike, bream, tench, rudd and roach. The bream run to 6lb. Day tickets are available at a cost of 30p. These can be obtained both from the club secretary and from G. Denny and Sons, Market Place, Harleston. The club takes bookings for matches on the pits.

From Shotford Bridge to Mendham Bridge the Norfolk bank is all controlled by the Harleston and Wortwell club. The roach stock has shown a radical improvement in recent years and is now almost at its best. It was in this area, above Mendham Bridge, that the first chub ever released in the Broads area as a whole were turned loose. The fish have bred and are firmly established, providing good sport which is usually at its best in the autumn through the winter to the season's end.

There are no bream this far upriver, but plenty of pike and some dace. The flow is usually quite light except after heavy rain. The Waveney here benefits from rain. It quickens the pace of the river and brings colour to the water which in turn makes the fish more responsive. Unfortunately the colour never stays long but the Waveney Valley as a whole has a tendency to flood, with the result that the flow rate will continue long after the colour has gone.

There are large numbers of tench through the whole length of the Waveney, but it is rare for really big fish to be caught. Catches of up to seven at a sitting are made each year, but most of the fish weigh 3lb or less. There are, of course, better ones for the catching and it is worth recording that a 7lb tench was taken from an eel trap at Ellingham some years ago. Mendham and Earsham are two of the more productive localities for tench and both places have yielded 5-pounders.

Below Homersfield bridge the river shallows very considerably. In places the water is only a few inches deep, running over a gravel bottom, and there are some excellent dace and chub in this length. The fish are usually taken from the deeper runs. To date no one has yet taken a dace of 1lb here and the top weight appears to be around the 12oz mark. At Homersfield the Black Swan Inn has 500 yards of the river which is retained exclusively for guests.

The Water Authority controls a length of the Waveney on the left-hand bank at Earsham. This extends over two and a half miles and details may be obtained locally at the Buck Inn, Earsham. This excludes one short length, known locally as the Buck Hills. The opposite bank at Flixton, from Buck Hills to the mill sluice, is controlled by the Bungay Cherry Tree AC and fishing on that side is for club members only.

The next area of importance is close to the town of Bungay where the river forms a huge horseshoe bend around Bungay Common. There are four miles of river here with anglers able to fish $2\frac{1}{2}$ miles of it. The remaining $1\frac{1}{2}$ miles is controlled by the Suffolk County AA and day tickets, price 50 pence, are available from A.A.Collen, 17 Commodore Road, Oulton Broad.

There is a long walk to the river across the common and Bungay Golf Course, with fine catches of roach the reward for those making the effort. There are also numbers of tench and chub.

The Waveney bank controlled by the Bungay Cherry Tree AC – with the exception of the Bungay Common length – is retained exclusively for club members, but anyone can join. The annual membership fee is £2.50, juniors 50p, and this can be considered inexpensive for a week's fishing in the club water. The club also has a well-stocked pit at Ditchingham containing quality coarse fish of the usual species.

Bungay Fleece AC controls one mile of the river upstream of The Maltings. No day tickets issued. The secretary is D. Marr, Mayfair Road, Bungay. Below the Maltings on the Suffolk side Bungay Cherry Tree controls a further two miles of the bank.

The Water Authority has the fishing rights over short stretches on both banks upstream of Wainford Mill and similar lengths on streams in the vicinity of the Maltings. Map supplied on request. These lengths contain the first bream in the Waveney. Like the shoals in the upper Bure, the fish run to a very good size, both above and below the mill. Seven-pounders are taken in most seasons and the weight ceiling appears to be around the 8lb mark.

Chub were put into the reach below Wainford Mill 18 years ago. They were good fish, some of them weighing 4lb when they were released. There were 2000 fish in the consignment. They came from the River Wissey and dropped down river from the area where they were introduced to make their presence felt at Ellingham.

This length fishes best when there is a fair degree of flow and some water colour. There are numbers of roach, with some 2lb fish present. The depth varies rather a lot. In some swims there is as little as 3ft and in others 10ft so it is important to choose a swim with care.

Bread is the best all-round bait for the bigger fish, although some anglers use lobworms successfully for the bream. Maggots and casters all take their share of the bigger roach. A number of bream hybrids are caught in this area, as well as small bream. Access to this length is best on the Suffolk side, but half way down the length to Ellingham Mill the bank is controlled by the Suffolk County AA and day tickets are not issued.

Swims below Ellingham Mill are some of the most productive for really big roach, and there is a regular crop of 2-pounders when fishing conditions are good. There are also a great many pike and, though the majority are small, a 27½lb fish was taken by an Ipswich angler in the 1950s. The mill pool area contains a number of large chub — and smaller ones. The biggest fish weigh comfortably in excess of 6lb.

The length on the Suffolk side extending downstream almost to Geldeston is also Suffolk County AC water, with no tickets available. Shoals of bream are to be found all through this length of the river, but the fish do not attain the size of the fish further up. Their top weight here appears to be around 4lb but heavy catches are made. A Beccles club contest was once won with over 90lb of bream, with excellent supporting weights on the same day.

The river is now tidal at Ellingham. Geldeston Lock has been removed, but Geldeston is the upper limit of navigation for the bigger boats. Good perch and roach have been taken here in the past, although there has been reduced

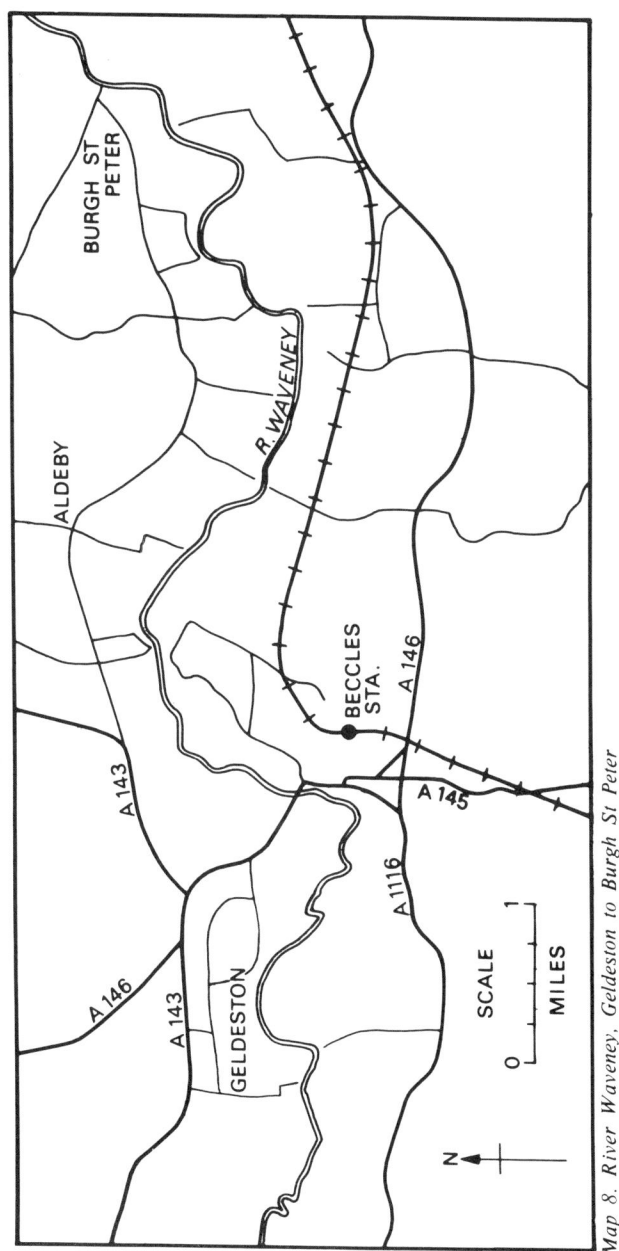

Map 8. River Waveney, Geldeston to Burgh St Peter

sport recently. A Yarmouth angler, J.M. Bunker, caught a roach of 2lb 11½oz here in the 1955/56 season. There is some Anglian Water Authority bank both above the lock on the Suffolk bank and downstream, again on the Suffolk side, extending to Beccles.

From below Geldeston to Beccles the river varies greatly in depth. In some swims there is as much as 16ft of water and, since it is often very clear, fishing can be rather patchy. Nevertheless, good catches of bream are usually made at Dunburgh, from the Norfolk bank. It was here that Tony Emden of Norwick took one of the biggest tench on record for the whole of Broadland in the summer of 1963. The tench weighed 6lb 9oz and was the only one Tony caught that day. More recently the same area produced the winning weight, 29lb of bream, in the 1976 Beccles Open Championship.

There is also some good bream fishing here, particularly early in the season when the fish are believed to move up from below Beccles. The Water Authority has the fishing rights on four miles of the south bank at Barsham, between Beccles and Shipmeadow. Access is via Pudding Lane and a farm road. This is free fishing to licence holders. Sections of the bank are swampy, but there is ample space for fishing. On the Norfolk bank, opposite to Barsham, the old River Authority — replaced by Anglian Water Authority — erected 15 wooden platforms to provide comfortable bank fishing. Access is via the woodyard upstream of the road bridge.

The most freely accessible bank fishing of all is below Beccles, where the Beccles AC administer a long stretch extending over two and a quarter miles on the Suffolk side. The lower limit is half a mile below the remains of what used to be the railway bridge before the line was closed and the bridge demolished. Individuals can fish as and when they wish without charge but visiting clubs must make prior application to the Beccles AC. The secretary is G. Kemp, 14 Marsh View, Beccles.

Fishing for pike can be very good in this area and it is one of the few lengths of river that produces 20-pounders with any regularity. These big fish have even been caught in the Corporation Cut at the yacht station.

Contests have been won with bream catches well in excess of 50lb and there are also good roach present. Many anglers fish this length with leger tackle but, while it undoubtedly produces many of the bigger bream catches, I always consider float fishing just as practical and possibly more enjoyable. It is a matter of individual preference. The main river is deep and has an average depth of 10ft and a

2½ ft rise and fall with the tide.

The best area for bream is undoubtedly three-quarters of a mile below Beccles, just above the first sharp bend. The fish are not big individually, running to 3½ lb, but there are a great many 2-pounders. This area gives its best results in the autumn and winter but two bends downstream there is another favourite spot. Inside the bend the water is shallower than that generally found and numbers of tench are taken in summer. Anglers who fish here at night will take some heavy nets of bream.

Anglers can also fish the Norfolk side of the river, where the length extending downstream to Boat House Hill is now Water Authority controlled. There is a path through to the left just before the main bridge over the river on the outskirts of Beccles on the Norwich road. This leads through to the river walk – there is almost unlimited space and the banks are in fine order.

Further downriver the bank becomes inaccessible, with thick reed growth into the edge of the river. The Water Authority has the fishing rights from a three-quarters of a mile length at Aldeby, and this is an excellent foothold into an area which, although unpredictable, contains both roach and bream – quantity and quality.

The Water Authority has the fishing rights of a 190 yard stretch immediately downstream of the road that touches the river below Worlingham Mill, on the Suffolk side. Float fishing is still possible here on favourable tides, but with the bream preferring a bait offered still on the bottom, legering becomes the more practical proposition. Best results follow heavy groundbaiting.

The North Cove and Barnby AC has 1½ miles between Worlingham and Barnby with parking space for six cars. Day tickets available from A. Crack, Fishing Tackle Dealer, Blyburgate, Beccles, and at the Post Office, Barnby.

The lower length from Worlingham past Burgh St Peter to the top of Oulton Dyke holds extremely heavy stocks of bream all through the summer and autumn. It was in this region that Ian Meickle won a local club contest with a remarkable catch of bream weighing 150lb. This was taken from a boat. Catches of 100lb used to be made regularly here but although catches are not now so prolific they continue to be good in the summer.

Local tactics are to leger with a heavy Arlesey bomb or coffin lead, using a large hook; size 10 to 6. The best baits are either bread paste or maggot. When using maggot it has been found that it pays to put as many as a dozen on the hook at a time!

There is some fine pike fishing in the river below

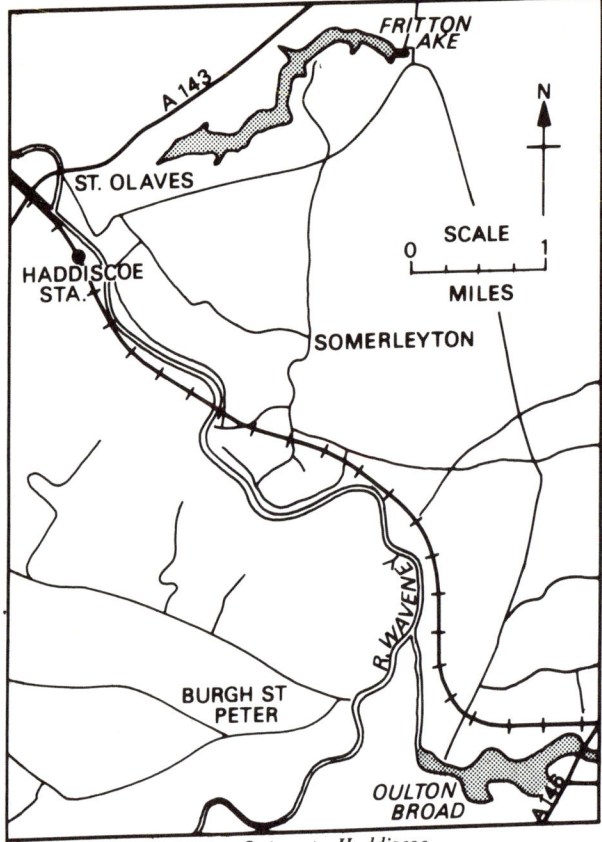

Map 9. River Waveney, Oulton to Haddiscoe

Worlingham to Burgh St Peter, despite the strength of the flow. Sam Searle, once the fishery bailiff, has had pike of 20lb and 21lb 4oz from this length. This area has never had much publicity as a pike fishery but is worth a visit. Anglers can expect catches of up to ten fish a day, but they are advised to take their livebait with them. Roach are difficult to catch here in the winter.

There is some bank fishing at Burgh St Peter but this is limited, and boats can be obtained both at Burgh St Peter and Oulton Broad. Tides are very strong and there is the occasional influx of salt water. However this usually comes in the winter and only very rarely in summer. Fortunately the fish always keep in front of the salt and there are never the large-scale fish mortalities that sometimes occur in the lower reaches of other Broadland rivers.

The one and a half miles of Oulton Dyke also provide good catches of bream, with many roach. It pays to fish from a boat and there is some access to the bank at Fishers Row by a footpath to the right of Oulton Broad.

Below Oulton Dyke's junction with the Waveney the main river has an even stronger flow but big shoals of fish are found all the way down to Somerleyton and Haddiscoe. Float fishing is rarely worth while and the only time it pays off are when anglers fish indentations in the bank that offer them some shelter from the main flow.

The New Cut, running from Haddiscoe to Reedham, is heavily fished in the summer. This too is fast running and legering is a must. Being man-made, its banks are straight and provide no slack water for float fishing. Principal stocks are of bream but there are also plenty of roach that run to a good average size. Two-pound roach are very rare here but there are large number of 8oz fish to give continuous sport.

Below Haddiscoe it is sometimes possible to catch good fish in the Waveney but the river here is only five miles from Breydon Water, the vast lake behind Great Yarmouth, always brackish and often completely salt. Anglers are more likely to catch smelts and flounders than freshwater fish and it is pointless to fish below Haddiscoe.

River Wensum

The Wensum, almost throughout its length, is a roach river first and foremost. Shoals of big fish are to be found almost everywhere and they run to well over the 2lb mark. The weight ceiling appears to be a little short of 3lb for, at least to date, a fish of that weight has never been reported caught. There is a high proportion of fish topping the 2lb mark and anglers have taken as many as nine of these fish in a single day – as well as heavy catches of fish over the 1lb mark.

If there is a snag with the Wensum from the coarse fisherman's angle it is that it is also a trout river. It has a better flow than the upper reaches of either the Bure and the Waveney and trout anglers have taken full advantage in some stretches. Some lengths are heavily stocked most years and, after such expense, the people who either own the banks or rent the rights are far from keen to share their sport with the man who fishes maggots for roach.

Yet with such heavy stocking it is inevitable that some of

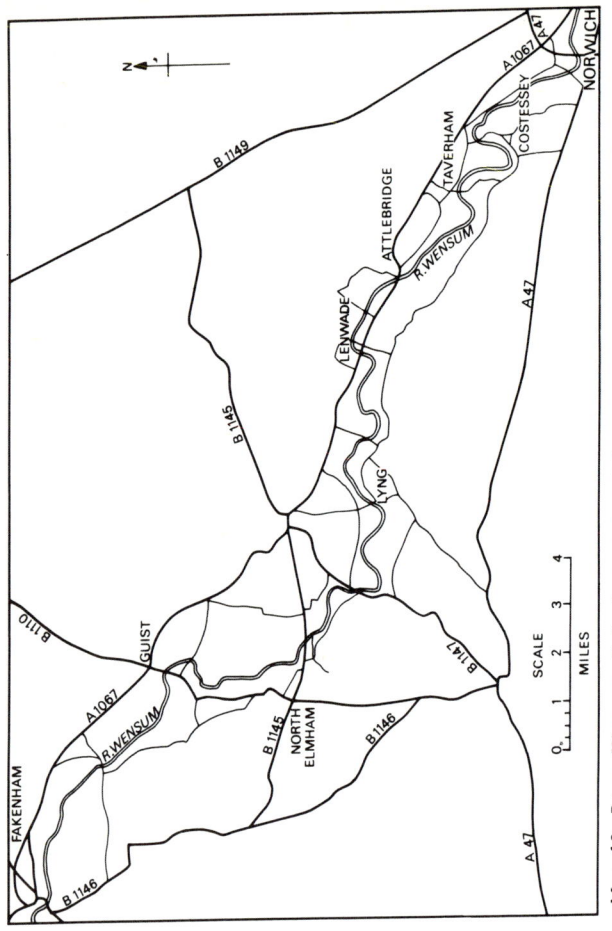

Map 10. River Wensum, Fakenham to Norwich

the trout should stray out of the private reaches and in most places there is always the chance for the man who fishes either fly, worm or lure for them. However, trout fishing is by fly only in the freshwater fish close season.

The most important development, in my view, has been the stocking with barbel. The numbers were small but two separate batches were introduced and there were enough fish in the stocking effort to provide a breeding nucleus. Barbel have been caught occasionally but it would be an exageration to imply that barbel fishing as such exists now. It doesn't.

But provided the 200 fish turned in have bred and can multiply these fish will provide an important step forward. Not only are barbel a most sporting species in their own right but they can extend the scope of the Wensum at a time when river traffic is making fishing difficult elsewhere. There is no boat traffic on the Wensum and since barbel are generally at their best in the summer months — when Wensum roach are less active — then the river could become more popular and provide peaceful fishing for those who want it.

The Wensum rises at West Rudham but is a trout water at first with little or no access for the general public until it has reached Fakenham — some eight river-miles away. The length immediately above Fakenham, extending to Sculthorpe has been stocked with trout by Fakenham Angling Association. Most of this length is private, but Len Bryer, the tackle dealer at Norwich Street, Fakenham, will give additional information to visitors who want to fish this area.

Anglers can obtain permission to fish the 300 yard stretch belonging to Dewing and Kersley, the millers. This holds good roach and dace, plus numbers of trout. Below this length there is a stretch some one and a half miles long running through common land at Fakenham. The river is shallow here with a depth of around 2ft. It is often very clear and is not easy to fish successfully. Nevertheless roach of 2lb are caught each year, along with trout that sometimes top the 3lb mark. The water though is gin clear here and the favourite tactics are to stalk the fish rather than attempt to feed them into a position where they can be caught. Anglers who walk the bank in full view of the fish catch very little.

A long length from Ryburgh road bridge down to Guist, some three miles in all, is an Anglian Water Authority controlled trout fishery. Day permits are issued from the East Suffolk and Norfolk Division Norwich office and cost £1.50 each. The stretch is stocked from time to time and exists in an area where trout have every chance of survival and of giving good sporting fishing with fly.

There is no fishing in nearby Sennowe Park lake – although this is known to contain a substantial stock of excellent roach. Some local anglers do fish it from time to time with the permission of the owner and have had catches in excess of 40lb, including roach to 2lb 8oz.

The Water Authority also controls some of the fishing above Bintry Mill. This can be fished on a 12½ pence permit obtained, like the trout permits, direct from the Divisional offices in Norwich. The biggest length extends over a mile on the right bank, ending just below the mill itself. On the left bank a 500 yard length is similarly available. This begins at the site of the old railway bridge and continues to within 150 yards of the mill. Access to the latter stretch is via the mill yard. The right bank is reached via a road signposted to Bintry on the main Dereham to Holt road.

Roach fishing is the best prospect. The fish are large – well over 2lb – but the general run of fish caught is in the 8oz to 1½ lb limits. There are also quantities of dace – and numbers of trout that have worked downstream from the trout fisheries further upriver.

It need be no real surprise to catch a bream here. There are not many, but the Dereham club turned some in years ago and a few of the progeny remain. There could be very big fish, perhaps weighing as much as 8lb each.

The dace run to better than 1lb. The best of them, unfortunately, are in a private length. The Water Authority has the fishing rights of several lengths in the vicinity of North Elmham. Three are by permit only, but there is one length of 1000 yards of the right bank, approached from a farm lane near North Elmham church, which is freely available to licence holders. Maps of the permit water are available from the authority headquarters in Norwich. The permits cost 12½ pence per day. Some of the dace in this general area are big fish, big for dace that is, but the stretch immediately below Billingford bridge is private.

Downstream to Swanton Morley much of the fishing is private but there are good roach, dace and pike here.

It was somewhere in this area – they declined to name the exact location–that a party of eleven Leicester anglers took a catch of more than 500lb of roach in a day in January, 1965. One man alone had 120lb and commented: 'The fish were so hungry they would have eaten my hat if they'd been given the chance!' The roach in this catch weighed up to, but not better than 2lb, and dace to 10oz were also caught.

On other occasions the same anglers have done very well with much bigger fish. Eddie Allen and George Elliott once had sixteen 2lb roach between them in a single day's fishing. These big catches are made on float fished maggots on the hook. The best roach reported here in recent years weighed 2lb 15oz. In 1964 a perch of 4lb 3oz was taken at Swanton Morley by an angler fishing for roach.

There are not a great number of perch in the Wensum but in some instances they do grow to a most respectable size. If there has been a temporary lapse of standard by these perch, it seems inevitable they will show again by the early 1980s if not before.

There are some good pike in these upper reaches and one catch of seventeen fish – the best a 14-pounder – was taken in 1965. There are believed to be much bigger pike in these Swanton Morley reaches and one angler, whose word I am quite prepared to accept, told me that he once saw a pike of 30lb lying dead at the water's edge.

The stretch between Elsing Mill and Lyng Mill has at times suggested it is the best in the whole river. It has a fabulous head of roach and it was just above Lyng Mill that Norwich angler Sid Baker once caught 154lb of roach in four and a half hours fishing. Sid legered with bread on a size 10 hook and in one spell had four 2lb roach in successive casts. He had five over the 2lb mark in his total and, while using two hooks at once, on seven occasions had fish of more than 1lb on both hooks.

There is now no public access to the river. The water is controlled by clubs, associations and individuals who make no provision for visitors by way of day tickets, but the Dereham club has one stretch at the village of Lyng, and visitors can become members of the club and thus fish the water.

There is also a large pit at Lyng controlled by the Dereham club. This too is for members only, but it has a fine stock of roach and some dace. The best prospect here is the tench fishing. In summer, catches of 40lb of these fish are often made. The fish are not small, and it is known that tench as big as 6lb are there to be caught. The pit has an average depth of between 8ft and 10ft. There is a car park available.

Access to the Dereham club's length of the Wensum here is by walking past the pit over the iron bridge, and across the meadow to the riverside.

The London Anglers' Association has a number of fisheries on the Wensum for which day tickets are not available. The LAA does, however, operate a scheme by which associate membership is available at a reduced fee.

This then allows individuals to fish the otherwise restricted stretches.

The London Association has two stretches at Lyng, both on the right bank. The limits of these, as of all LAA fisheries, are clearly defined by notice boards. One short length is downstream of the Lenwade road out of Lyng, the other and bigger stretch is upstream. Neither is adjacent to the road bridge and cannot be approached by walking along the river bank.

Day tickets are though issued for Station Lakes, Great Witchingham Lakes, and Bridge Lakes, all at Lenwade and all of them London AA waters. The LAA also has 700 yards of Wensum bank, access point Walsis Farm, at Lenward but this is a members-only water.

The Wensum in this sector is rather more varied. It is shallow below Lenwade bridge and dace are numerous. Elsewhere it is the roach that again offer the bulk of the sport. The depth tend to vary but deeper holes and swims exists where there is 5ft of water. Occasionally much deeper holes can be located.

These deeper areas, as distinct from narrow and deeper swims, will fish well when the river is running strongly, after heavy rain but under normal conditions the fish tend to be out and about in the river where it is shallower.

Bread, caster and maggot baits each take good quality fish and there is little to choose between them in efficiency in the overall sense, but there are days when one will outscore the other two.

The length below Lenwade through to Attlebridge is in the hands of trout syndicates and there is no real access for visiting coarse fishermen. There is though one short length of 150 yards on the right above Ringland bridge and a shorter length on the right where coarse fishing is permitted.

The river is shallow here and is good dace water. The roach are perhaps rather less numerous here but there are numbers of trout. In addition there are both chub and grayling. The grayling are not now very numerous but the chub are increasing both in size and numbers. The trout can be large through this area and fish weighing up to $6\frac{1}{4}$ lb are caught from time to time.

Between Ringland and Taverham most of the fishing is again in private hands. Immediately below Taverham bridge the Water Authority has an 800-yard length of the right bank, known as The Nurseries. On the same bank and below The Nurseries stretch the Authority also has what is known as The Falcon length. This is named after a public house no longer in operation and covers some 500 yards.

This area of the river contains some above average pike, fish topping 20lb are caught from time to time and the best since the last war is a 28-pounder. With the pike so large it figures that the food fish stock is also good and roach and dace are numerous all the way downstream to Costessey Mill. The chub in this area are of excellent quality. Six-pounders have been taken and there is some chance of even bigger fish.

The chub are even more numerous on the downstream side of the mill and through Drayton to Hellesdon. This length received the biggest number of the chub put into the river and it is here that barbel were also released.

Much of this length is shallow and densely-weeded in the summer. The best results with both chub and roach are made after frost has knocked the weed down and when the flow rate and water colour has increased. During summer the peak times are at first and last light each day, when minimal daylight helps to offset the clarity of the water and the fish are therefore rather less shy and more likely to feed.

The 'fish farm' built by the East Suffolk and Norfolk River Authority is located above Hellesdon Mill on land on the south bank between the Wensum and its tributary the Tud. Not only has this fish farm been an expensive flop but it has robbed anglers of the opportunity to fish the adjacent bank, where the chub and roach fishing can be of high quality.

The Tud is a shallow stream but contains a better head of fish than its appearance might suggest. There are quality roach—some over 2lb—dace over 12oz and chub in it at this point.

There are no restrictions on fishing below Hellesdon mill, or the area past the Gatehouse Inn to Boundary road bridge. Hellesdon mill pool is known to contain some sizable barbel and, hopefully, may contain many more smaller ones as well as chub and the occasional very big brown trout.

This is a very accessible area offering roach, dace, tench and some good pike through its length. The Norwich to Hellesdon road runs parallel to the river and is at most little more than 100 yards away from the water.

Below Boundary bridge there is easy access and free fishing all the way downstream on the left bank to Wensum Park. The right bank has either limited access or is restricted. A substantial number of tench were released here some years ago but these fish don't now appear to be so numerous as they were ten years ago. Having said that, no-one should be surprised if he catches tench for there are a number remaining. Local opinion is that this length could be improved to become an outstanding and extremely useful fishery but mismanagement of the water level, particularly at spawning time, has imposed severe restrictions which the fishery managers have done nothing to ease.

From Dolphin bridge to City New Mills, where the river becomes tidal, access is very limited. Some of it can be fished only from a boat. The river has deepened considerably here and some swims have over 10ft of water. There are some but not many bream in this length.

New Mills pool has a stock of virtually everything the Wensum has to offer. There are some barbel, chub, a large number of pike, some of them big ones, and roach and dace. This area is virtually inaccessible other than by boat but roach are numerous through the Fye Bridge length, where there is known to be a big shoal of bream running to over 5lb. From time to time the fish in this area, in the heart of Norwich, suffer losses from pollution of various kinds but the quality of the fishing never seems to suffer a serious setback on that account.

In this tidal area the roach are not of such a high average weight as exists in the middle Wensum but 2lb roach are there to be caught. The main stock though is of roach running to $1\frac{1}{2}$lb, with the 4oz to 6oz fish apparently more common in this tidal river than in any other area.

The area each side of Foundry bridge provides a very popular local match venue with the results good enough in winter to attract anglers from the East Midlands. Match weights usually top the 20lb mark and catches in excess of 50lb have been known. The roach though can be finnicky. A change of tide can kill their appetites and anglers who had been taking fish in rapid succession are sometimes left with the impression that the fish have disappeared altogether.

Norwich Yacht Station occupies the area immediately above Foundry bridge and this area is virtually unfishable in summer because of the congestion and disturbance from boats moored there. A shoal of bream is usually in residence immediately below Foundry bridge but along the Riverside road length roach are the primary species.

This area, although markedly more attractive than in past years, is hardly a scenic delight but the roach fishing is of such high quality from autumn onward that the banks are usually well populated with anglers. When the fish are prepared to feed the fishing is really quite easy and this is a popular section for local youngsters.

Roach and some bream are to be found all the way

through the remaining length of the river past the now derelict power station to the point where the Wensum loses its identity as it merges with the much smaller River Yare.

There is no real access for the general public to this lower area but boat fishing can produce some really outstanding weights of both bream and roach. There are known to be some carp in this area but the fish are rarely caught and with the power station closed down there seems less chance of these fish being caught in the future.

Wroxham Broad

This 120-acre water is controlled by the Norfolk Broads Yacht Club. It can be fished by boat all through the season but there is only one tiny piece of bank available for shore fishing. This is reached from Wroxham Village and is situated just before the clubhouse and moorings of the sailing club.

The broad varies considerably in depth, the deeper water being on the far side of the broad, close to the River Bure. The extreme ends are both shallow, but it is usually from these places, where the depth is less than 6ft, that the best catches of bream are made. The deeper water will yield good nets of roach in the summer months, with a high proportion of the fish topping 8oz and running to over 2lb. I have always found bread the best bait on this water, but bream anglers have had heavy catches using worm.

It pays to fish for the bream quite close to lily or weedbeds. The water is often quite clear and the bream seem to spend much of their time in thick vegetation. Sport does not always come at once and I have found it best to fish for at least an hour before looking for another swim. Swims close to weed need groundbaiting but not in such quantity as in the deeper places.

My favourite spot for roach is on the far side of the broad immediately opposite the headquarters of the sailing club. This is also a favourite for pike in the autumn and winter but, at the same time, it can often disappoint.

As a pike water the broad is something of an enigma. Fish of 20lb are taken there each winter but the broad rarely produces fish like the heavyweights that came so regularly from Heigham Sound. The extreme ends of the broad provide good numbers of average sized pike to all methods.

The water might have come up with one huge pike some years ago if the late Sid Baker of Norwich had been more fortunate with a fish he and his companion estimated to be in the 35lb class. The pike took a spoon, but the anglers had only a landing net with them and, when an attempt was made to bag the fish, the net fouled on one set of treble hooks outside the pike's jaw and the fish escaped.

Although few tench are taken, there are good numbers of these fish present. Late-night groundbaiting in a raked swim could give sport for early morning summer anglers but, regrettably, I have yet to hear of any outstanding successes.

Best results with the bottom-feeding species are in the summer and early autumn. With the first hard frosts all species—pike excepted—seem to disappear, but with prolonged mild weather these fish are caught there in winter, so it must be that the fish pass into semi-hibernation rather than leave the broad altogether.

Wroxham Broad gives perhaps the best example of the widespread silting taking place on the still and slow-moving waters. After the last war I was annoyed by a comment in another book on Norfolk Broads fishing which suggested the broad was 26ft deep at maximum depth. So I took the trouble to establish its precise depth.

At normal level there was 13ft 6in of water on the Bure side, opposite the yacht clubhouse. In 1971, some 20 years later the depth had changed drastically. Maximum was then 9 ft 6in. I haven't measured it since but I should not be surprised at a reading of $8\frac{1}{2}$ ft.

This shallowing process is the result of the heavy river traffic. The wave action has eroded the banks and washed them into the river. As the result we now have bigger but shallower waters almost everywhere.

Were it not for the fact that the Bure banks are either close piled or held together by the roots of the alder trees the banks would probably have eroded even further than they have already. A major problem is developing here.

Salhouse Broad

This broad is an almost exact miniature of Wroxham Broad. It is located off the Bure midway between Wroxham and Woodbastwick and, like Wroxham, has two entrances to the main river.

The deepest water—once 10ft but now 8ft—is at the Woodbastwick end but the bulk of the broad is much shallower. A large section of bank can be fished from but

Wind direction

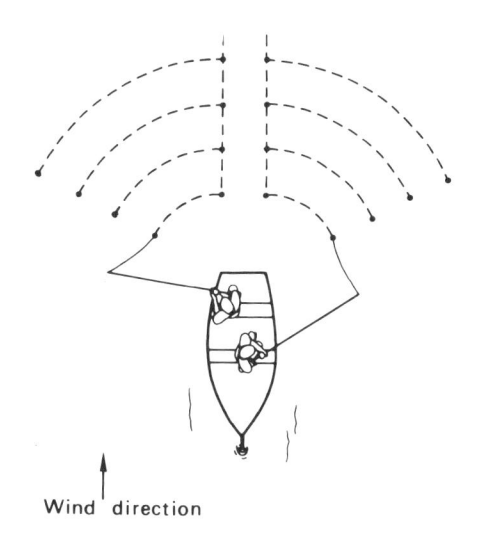

This drawing shows how two anglers livebaiting for pike from a boat can effectively cover the water around them. Note the boat is moored by the bow only. This not only ensures that each angler has an equal opportunity, it also means that a big pike cannot run beneath the boat and foul the line around the ropes or poles. Each cast is made across the wind at varying distances and the wind works the bait down and in, thus covering the water.

charges are made for this, for mooring and for boat fishing.

The broad contains numbers of all the indigenous broads species, with roach and bream the most numerous. There are some tench, perch and pike but the pike do not as a rule compare with those from Wroxham Broad. Some of the Salhouse reputation for big pike is false. Hoveton Great Broad is only 200 yards away on the opposite side of the Bure and some anglers have fished the Great Broad, caught big pike and given the credit to Salhouse!

From time to time 20lb pike are taken from it but most of the fish seem limited to around 15lb. This is a good night fishing water for bream, in summer over heavily-baited swims. Again bread, used either as paste or flake, has the happy knack of picking out the bigger fish.

The bank fishing is nothing to rave over since the adjacent water is relatively shallow but it can be productive early in the day. In 1963, all against the form, a local angler caught a roach of 3lb 5oz there. He had several other roach over 2lb and a number of bream between 2lb and 3lb on the same day.

Woodbastwick Decoy Broad

Decoy Broad is connected to the Bure by a shallow, narrow dyke and there is no access for boats from the main river. It is a private water with the fishing controlled by the Norwich and District AA. This is a members-only water but since anyone can join the association no one is really excluded. Membership enquiries to Cliff Braithwaite, 4, Cranage Road, Lakenham, Norwich (telephone Norwich 25682). The present membership fee is £1.50 but since the boats cost only 75 pence per day to hire this means that a day's fishing costs only £2 at the most!

The broad is fished regularly by local clubs who organize boat fishing contests through the summer and although results are never predictable the bream show regularly enough to provide excellent match weights topping 20lb. Boats are maintained on the broad through the winter when pike fishing produces some good fish. The best on record is the 29-pounder taken in 1975 by water authority bailiff Dan Leary.

Fish of this size are, of course, exceptional, but the broad is well-stocked with pike running into double figures.

The broad is a mixture of shallow and quite deep water. Maximum depth is around 10ft but in daylight many of the bream are caught in the shallow areas where the water is heavily festooned with lily beds. There is no bank fishing.

The roach, as on most stillwater broads, are usually on the small side but this is a quiet summer sanctuary where anglers can fish in peaceful surroundings and have the water to themselves.

Hoveton Little Broad

This water, often known as Black Horse Broad, covers some 80 acres and is open to boat traffic in the summer but closed in winter. The fishing is private. The entrance to the broad runs into the Bure three-quarters of a mile upstream of Horning.

Some members of the Norfolk and Suffolk Yacht Owners' Association — now Blakes, a booking agency for broads boating holidays — forced their way through the entrance after the Second World War to try to bring about a legal test case to establish that the water was in fact public on the basis that it is tidal. There was no clear result and the outcome was a compromise under which boats have since been allowed on the broad throughout the summer.

The water holds large stocks of pike and although few anglers can obtain permission to fish, 20-pounders are caught from time to time. There are also many bream, rudd and tench.

Ranworth Maltsters and Inner Broads

Malthouse Broad, reached from the Bure via Ranworth Dyke, is shallow and silted. It is a very popular mooring place for holiday craft and is used to such an extent in summer that the fishing gets only a low rating.

It contains pike, bream and roach, with early morning and night fishing providing the only chance of worthwhile catches. Some bream can be caught on those rare days when the broad is quiet.

It is a better proposition in the autumn when bream can sometimes be found in strong shoal strength by anglers fishing from the staithe. Boats to fish this broad and Ranworth Dyke itself can be hired near the staithe.

The Inner Broad is private but the fishing is controlled by the Norwich and District AA. Fishing is not allowed from September 30 until March 1. The Norwich Association operates a fleet of fishing boats on the inner broad and these can be booked either via association secretary Cliff Braithwaite, 4, Cranage Road, Norwich (telephone Norwich 25682) or Norwich tackle dealers. Full association membership, present fee £1.50, allows visitors to book the Norwich boats at the exceptionally low cost of 75 pence per day. Non-members pay 25 pence per rod plus the boat hire fee.

During the summer the inner broad produces good catches of bream with some roach and a few tench but peak activity come from March 1 when the broad reopens to allow anglers the chance of fishing for the pike. Pike are numerous and some of them are big. Twenty pounders come most years. Some of the best of these fish are taken from the middle of the broad, with deadbaits, herring in particular, doing well.

South Walsham Broads

Boats have access to both the outer and inner broads but only the former is open to fishing. There is little or no bank fishing other than on the nearby Fleet Dyke, which connects the broads to the Bure.

The outer broad offers bream and pike fishing, with some roach, but this is a shallow water with, unfortunately, the best fishing found in the inner broad. The area is heavily used by boat traffic in summer – which restricts its performance – but after-dark fishing both from a boat and from the bank at Fleet Dyke can yield heavy bream catches.

Barton Broad

Barton Broad, extending over 200 acres, has often been described as the most attractive of all the broads. It is shallow all over, with a depth of no more than 6ft, with much of it at only 3ft.

Due to the fact that the water is usually well-coloured, the weed growth is not so profuse as on Hickling, but the water is lined with reeds along most of the edges and there are some dense patches of summer growth. At its downstream end the broad is almost divided into two by Pleasure Hill Island but there is a navigable channel at each side of the island.

At one time the broad had an outstanding reputation for big pike and fish of 20lb and more were caught regularly between the wars. There remains a very good head of pike on the water even though 20-pounders are not taken as regularly as perhaps might be the case. I believe there are still substantial numbers of really big pike on the water. The food fish exist in quantity and there is no reason why 30-pounders should not be taken. The last such fish from Barton was caught by Dennis Pye in August 1962, when he also had a 28lb fish.

The best pike are usually taken close to the reeds with some of the better quality pike showing near the lower junction of the broad with the Ant. But the continued failure to catch the biggest of the pike suggests that traditional thinking may be best forgotten and it could pay to concentrate on areas that are little fished.

In the summer months some of the best bream, tench and rudd catches are made in the lily-beds and weeds that go to make up what locals call 'The Jungle'. This is on the left of the broad above the island. The best results – as in so much of Broadland – are usually made before breakfast, but the smaller bream can be expected to feed right through the day. There is nothing unusual in catches on the 50lb mark in summer, although there is the tendency for the bream to be of only average size. Nevertheless the bigger fish of up to 3lb have been caught in greater numbers recently.

All fishing on the broad has to be by boat since the banks are inaccessible. These can be hired either at the Cox Bros boatyard at Barton Turf or from The Barton Angler Hotel, Irstead. This hotel is unique in Broadland in that it specializes in catering for anglers and is open throughout the fishing season.

The hotel is situated close to Gay's Staithe in Neatishead Dyke; to the left of the island for anglers approaching upstream from the Ant. The dyke has an average depth of around 4ft and also holds a fine head of fish. Bream and rudd are the best prospect although there are huge stocks of roach and good numbers of tench. As a matter of personal choice I would just as soon fish this dyke for bream as any other part of the broad.

The dyke does get a degree of boat traffic in summer, from craft passing to the mooring staithe at the extreme end at Neatishead, but this has little effect on the fishing. In winter it holds even more fish than in summer and is well worth a visit. At that time of the year the dyke holds large numbers of rudd and it is possible to pick out some of the bigger ones by fishing with bread, as a change from maggots.

The bream concentrations found in winter at the extreme upper limit of Neatishead dyke have to be fished for to be fully believed. The massed shoals are extremely dense. The fish are not necessarily big ones, bream of $1\frac{1}{2}$ lb predominate, but roach are there too and these also weigh to $1\frac{1}{2}$ lb.

Similar concentrations are also found in the wide dyke at Barton Turf. The broad's bream have this tendency to congregate into very localized areas during the cold weather and this is not peculiar to Barton Broad. It also happens at the upper end of Stalham Dyke and in some of the

Wroxham and Horning boat basins. Catches made in these places are often far and away better than the weather conditions on the day suggest are possible.

Pike are also prolific, as is only to be expected, in Neatishead dyke in winter. They can obviously be expected to follow their food-fish and single day sessions can yield up to ten fish. Fifteen pounds seems the ceiling weight.

Perch were once numerous but in common with all Broadland their numbers diminished in the mid 1960s. Happily the little perch are back in force and given time the bigger ones must show again, probably from 1980.

Barton has never been rated as an outstanding tench prospect but there are good numbers of the fish on the broad. I have known anglers to get up to six in a session with the best fish weighing in at just over 4lb. We have never seen the best of these fish here.

It may be right to suggest that too many anglers lose heart too quickly. They chase the fish instead of letting the fish come to them. The best way has to be to select a favourable area, one close to reed or weed out of the summer boat traffic and to groundbait it heavily.

The bream and tench may not show first time but persevere. Feed it again... and again... and unless something is wrong with the choice of swim the bream must show. This is swim-preparation Irish style.

Lots of groundbait over a period will move a shoal in and hold it in place. If you can accept that this happens you will realize that to keep seeking new places in the hope of finding a resident shoal is much like chasing rainbows. Impatient anglers don't give themselves much chance of big bags.

Heigham Sound

Anglers of long standing need no introduction to Heigham Sound. This small piece of water, no larger than some of the bays on Hickling Broad, has produced a spate of specimen fish year after year. It is exceptionally shallow and very heavily weeded in summer, except in the narrow boat channel. This channel is clearly defined by marker posts and, as the result, the main sections of the open water are completely free from boat traffic. The only craft to venture on to it are shallow-draught dinghies and fishing boats.

This is not an easy water to fish. It is a mass of reeds and weeds in summer and the water is often very clear, with only the occasional break in the weeds offering a place to fish. But Heigham Sound cannot be measured by the standards applied to other waters. Many of the bigger fish are taken from the very edges of the weeds.

But the shadow of prymnesium hangs over the Sound. When this algal organism first occurred in Meadow Dyke, it spread down the dyke and over Heigham Sound. Large numbers of the Heigham stock fish escaped by fleeing into the River Thurne via Candle Dyke. Few dead fish were found on the water or on nearby Duck Broad.

Prymnesium is a plant organism which thrives in water possessing a high salt content. There have been only three previous known instances of it in the British Isles, although there have been upsets to fisheries in Israel, Holland and Bulgaria which have been attributed to prymnesium. This organism thrives on bright sunlight and multiplies at a staggering rate. But when the sun is sheathed by cloud the prymnesium dies. And when it dies it releases a toxin into the water which can be lethal to fish.

It may well be that there have been instances of prymnesium in the area before but, if there were, it escaped identification. But there have been large-scale mortalities in the past from which the fisheries have recovered quite quickly.

It seems that shoal fish have by far the best survival ratio and this is not too difficult to understand. When concentrations of roach and bream first begin to feel they are in trouble there is a shoal reaction and the shoal as a mass then tries to find a way of escape as disquiet spreads. Bream are known to have quite sensitive migratory instincts when trouble brews. They run ahead of the salt water surges in the lower Bure, for example. They are therefore quite well equipped to move out, even though some of the fish in each shoal may become affected before the alarm factor prevails. This is also true of the roach.

It cannot though be true of the species that tend to live most of their lives out as individuals – the pike, tench and eels. Pike and tench do congregate at times, mainly for spawning and on occasions when their food is in a concentrated area, but they are not shoal fish. So individual fish can be affected and succumb without necessarily passing their distress on to others of their species. So the mortality rate of pike, tench and eels was very much higher than with other species.

Even now we can't be sure what happened to the rudd. All the upper Thurne areas of still water contained fine stocks of these fish. Many 2-pounders and fish of 3lb and more used to be taken annually. These fish are no longer in

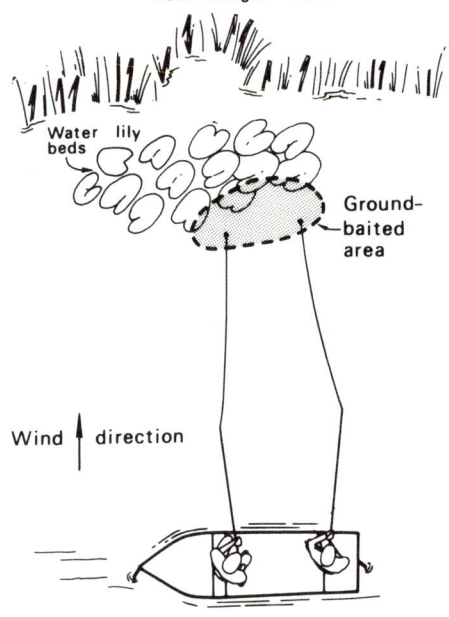

When float fishing on a stillwater the boat should be moored across the wind, using poles or dropweights at both the bow and the stern. The boat then maintains a fixed position and this ensures that the floats are not dragged out of position as the boat moves. Note that some groundbait has been thrown into the lilybed so that some bream can be held 'in reserve'. If the fish in the clear water become frightened these in the weeds are less likely to flee. Boats can also be moored across the stream in this manner – river traffic allowing, that is. Then two anglers can both trot float tackle downstream with the flow. On the other hand if the boat is moored bow upstream, stern downstream only the angler sitting in the stern can work float tackle down-river ... unless the boat is moored in mid-stream!

evidence, although insignificant numbers of tiny fish have been taken in isolated instances.

It figures then that the bream and roach fishing had to be the least affected and so it has proved. The summer of 1976, long, hot, often windless days, provided the high water temperature that prevailed from June through to mid-September. And even in October heavy bream weights continued to show all over the stillwaters of the upper Thurne area as a whole.

So, while acknowledging that prymnesium remains a threat, there is no need for excessive gloom. Catches of 100lb to a rod in one session are still on the cards for anglers who fish the right place at the right time. Heavy groundbaiting is essential and I have always found that the period immediately after dawn is the best time.

To get the really outstanding catches it pays to arrive on the water by boat (there is no bank fishing) late the previous evening. Select the swim with some care and feed it heavily. Ideally the swim needs to be located close to lily or other weedbeds. Groundbait is thrown into the leading edges of the weed as well as into the open water from which the fish will be hooked.

The idea here is that although the fish that venture out of the weed growth will be relatively easy to scare those within the weeds will feed away quite happily, not suspecting that anything is wrong. There is, therefore, a much reduced chance that the fish will take fright and flee once they have arrived in the swim.

It is better too to feed heavily at night rather than do the feeding first thing after dawn when the fish are most likely to be driven out of the swim by the commotion... which will have been long forgotten if it was done the previous evening.

Fishing through the night can produce bream catches- and does. Yet the best of the activity from bream comes when the darkness begins to lift and the first suggestions of daylight show in the sky. From that point the fish can be expected to feed in the grand style... and may well continue to feed right through to the middle of the morning and even beyond.

Much depends on the number of fish lost from the hook, the success or otherwise of your swim-feeding tactics and the size of the shoal. Catches of 1000lb of bream and more have been made in a week's fishing but there is a need for caution. Huge catches of bream are at risk if they are contained in keepnets for long periods.

It is selfish in the extreme to fill a keepnet to the brim with fish that suffer discomfort as the result. And if the water temperature is high then losses are inevitable. No keepnet should contain more than 50lb of bream for more than four hours.

So, if you must make a heavyweight catch, use more than one net... and never retain the fish from one day to the next. Once the session has ended turn all the fish loose.

Remember these are the stock fish that will provide the sport for the years tnat follow. The standard of future sport depends on these big fish having successful spawning years to help maintain the numbers of small fish growing on to specimen size.

These bream are usually the bigger ones. They can weigh to beyond 5lb and can be taken best of all on bread baits. My best session, made some years ago in company with Potter Heigham tackle dealer Ken Latham, scaled 124lb. It would have been higher had I not lost some 50lb of fish off the hook due to underwater snags. The fish were still feeding in the swim when we packed up fishing.

Tackle needs to be strong. Remember you will be fishing in shallow but heavily weeded water and you need to control each fish quickly- if only to ensure that it doesn't scare the remainder of the fish in the shoal. A 6lb line and a size 8 hook is by no means too heavy for this early morning fishing — although it would be daft to fish with such tackle in daylight in the rivers or even in stillwaters on unprepared swims.

Deep Dyke, connecting Heigham with Hickling, and Meadow Dyke, linking Heigham with Horsey, are both favoured bream sites for after dark fishing. Deep Dyke in particular has seen some enormous catches in summer. There is a limited amount of bank fishing here- although it can only be approached by boat- and this bank is extremely popular.

Meadow Dyke is not quite so good but it has been dredged comparatively recently. It therefore holds bream right through the autumn, as well as roach. It can give some fair fishing in the autumn when the boat traffic has eased and when there is then comfortable fishing in what is really quite a narrow water.

Roach are not nocturnal in the way that bream are. They can, of course, be caught during the night, but as a rule they are less active. In any case roach fishing is much more sporting and enjoyable in daylight, I think. Two pound roach can though be taken at night. Not many, of course, but there's always the chance of a big fish or two, particularly if the fishing site is in slightly flowing rather than absolutely still water.

Heigham Sound once contained a massive head of tench. More than Hickling Broad, more than Horsey, in relation to their respective sizes. Alas this isn't true any more and we can only hope that some intelligent work by the fishery authority will see some attempt at restoration.

I can confidently predict that the pike are coming back. The water was once so outstanding, everything about it is right for a big pike population, that these fish must return with time.

The biggest pike on record from the water is the 35lb 8oz fish landed by A. Jackson, of Hemsby, in December 1948. I saw that fish and what a magnificent specimen it was. Exceptionally deep in the body, it was undoubtedly of the stuff that record breakers are made. From time to time small pike showing this characteristic are caught through the Broads pike fisheries. They are short, stocky fish with a weight far in excess of what one normally expects for a given length. These are the fish I feel have the best chance of growing on to 30lb and more.

There's not much point in killing any pike, there's even less in killing one of these fish.

Heigham Sound pike often take up residence in the reedbeds that fringe the outer edges of the water. The reed walls are dense in places and although there is often only a few inches of water the pike stay within the reeds until moving out to feed.

Anyone who may doubt this should take a small dinghy into the reeds and he will see enough fish to confirm the truth of what I have said. Baits fished close to the edge of the reedbeds often produce good fish, sometimes later in the day, as the pike move out to have their feed before nightfall.

The best method for catching the pike is undoubtedly live-baiting. Many fish used to be caught on spoons and plugbaits. Keen as he is on these methods, Ken Latham, as enthusiastic a pike angler as ever fished the water, has had to admit that he gets a very large proportion of smaller fish for every specimen. Ken has had a number of 20lb plus fish and I saw him take one on a day when livebaiting proved unsuccessful for a lot of anglers.

Spare a thought for the pike when you catch one. Don't gaff it unless you really have to and, when removing the hooks, don't give an immature fish the full weight of the spring of the gag. This can so easily dislocate the fish's jaw. Many pike have been returned to the water by well-intentioned anglers but have subsequently died through being badly handled. Even the best of pike fishing can be ruined in time by continued bad handling of the fish.

One interesting point has come to light as the result of the tagging of pike by anglers acting for the River Authority. A number tagged on Heigham Sound have later been caught on Horsey Mere. Whether or not there is a migration from one water to the other is not conclusively known but, on the basis of these catches, there certainly seems to be considerable movement by the fish from one water to another.

Although the River Authority owns much of the bank around Heigham Sound it is impossible to approach the water's edge and there is no bank fishing whatsoever.

Hickling Broad

Hickling Broad, like Heigham Sound, lost a lot of fish in the 1969 prymnesium disaster but has made the same recovery. Bream and roach are there in strength but pike, tench and rudd have a way to go before they in any way rival the former stock.

It says a lot for this incredibly fertile fishery that among the pike found dead in 1969 was one fish measuring 49½ inches long. That fish could not have weighed less than 42lb and would most likely have weighed several pounds more. So it was without question a British record pike. Others estimated to be on or very close to the 40lb mark were also found dead at that time.

To help avert any possible recurrence of these losses in the future the fishery authority has established a bore hole and pump in a dyke leading off Catfield Dyke at the upper end of the broad. This pump has a capacity of some 750,000 gallons per day. The object is to provide a continuing supply of clean fresh water into the head of the broad and thus to provide a fish sanctuary if prymnesium ever returns in massive proportions.

Since prymnesium-free zones established themselves at Waxham Cut and in the Upper Thurne in 1969 it seems this scheme could very well do the job intended. Fish trapped at the extreme end of the broad will in future be attracted to this clean water where they must have a very good chance of survival. It could hardly be expected to save the lot but it would certainly ensure the survival of a very worthwhile breeding nucleus of fish of all ages and species.

There are between 400 and 500 acres of this, the largest of the Norfolk Broads. Most of it is very shallow and has a hard bottom with extensive weed-beds in summer, particularly in the vast sections never covered by the legions of motor cruisers. It is the shallowness of the broad that keeps much of it exclusively for angling. Boats are bound to the channel between the marker posts and only shallow-draft boats can venture outside the posts without running aground.

There is no bank fishing whatsoever on the broad itself although angling is possible from the boat moorings near the Pleasure Boat Inn.

The water is sometimes very clear and this means difficult fishing for roach, bream, tench and rudd. The clear-water areas are best fished early and late in the day, to liberal dosings of groundbait, but fish can be taken during midday periods.

On an ebb tide the flow takes clear water out of the broad but when it changes to flood the incoming water is coloured, particularly in the summer months. When this influx of colour sweeps into the broad it moves principally down the boat channel. This colour gets the fish feeding.

Moor a boat on the edge of the channel and cast float tackle into it. The fish will feed as long as the upstream flow lasts but once the tide changes and the colour fades sport may come to an end. While the colour lasts all the different species can be taken from the same swim. I remember telling that famous match angler Billy Lane of four casts I made in succession to the same spot using the same bait – bread flake – each time. The first cast produced a rudd of 2lb, the second a tench of $3\frac{1}{2}$lb. The third brought in a roach of 14oz and the fourth, a $1\frac{1}{2}$lb bream. Billy could only say: What were you fishing for?

That is the beauty of this sort of fishing. You can never tell what fish you will catch next. But for all its fine stock it can be a heart-breaker. Many anglers fish it convinced that everything will be all too simple. It doesn't work out that way. Success is rarely instantaneous.

Hickling's reputation as a rudd fishery was once as big as its reputation for pike. In high summer the fish used to be located in the shallowest of the reed-fringed bays. Dennis Pye once took a 3-pounder from a swim less than 12 inches deep!

Some of the best of this rudd fishing was located in Heigham Corner, a quiet and preserved section of the broad. There water is often very clear, with every detail of the bottom visible to the eye. In such conditions it is often well nigh impossible to catch fish out in the open water. The fish are in and close to the weed and reed and you catch them by casting a bait as close to the vegetation as can be managed.

I fished Heigham Corner on one occasion after the 1969 problem. The water was quite coloured on that occasion. I was on holiday and wasn't fishing seriously. Certainly I hadn't my full range of tackle and bait with me. In truth I hadn't expected to catch much, even if I bothered to fish at all.

After catching a prolonged sequence of tiny roach on maggot the fish eventually became bigger and then, after a run of no more than average sized roach, in came the bream. I had 14 bream up to 3lb and lost a couple to near successive casts- all on single or double maggot, fished on a small hook. That won't work in clear water but it does illustrate what can be accomplished when the water is coloured, as is the case in the boat channel extending from Deep Dyke and almost to the Pleasure Boat Inn at Hickling.

It was close to Hickling Pleasure Boat that three anglers from Doncaster had what must surely be one of the biggest bream catches over made anywhere. In three night's fishing they caught 1,200lb of fish on bread and maggot baits, the heaviest bream topping the 4lb mark.

I believe Hickling to be more difficult to fish than either Heigham Sound or Horsey Mere. Horsey has more colour and depth, Heigham Sound more colour, and these are the two key factors. If you can find a little more depth than the average — and coloured water to go with it — you can have wonderful sport. It therefore pays to spend a little time sorting out possibilities. If in fact I were new to this water and I was having a week's fishing on it I would spend the first day finding likely spots to fish. That time would be well spent.

There are good numbers of roach on Hickling and they run to a reasonable size. Pound fish are by no means uncommon and if few specimens are caught it may well be that no one, even now, has spent enough time and research in trying to seek out the bigger fish. It is in any case difficult to be single-minded about roach when there are so many bream to try for. Nevertheless 2-pounders have been caught on the broad in summer. In the winter the wide open waters of Hickling have little to offer. The shoals of bottom-feeding fish seem to melt away.

An east wind is not generally favourably regarded by broads anglers but it does bring one main advantage in its wake. An east wind reduces the water-levels of the broad and when the water in the reed-beds drains away pike are sometimes forced to move out into deeper water. At such times anglers can at least offer them a bait.

Strong wind is also often favourable. Some anglers subscribe to the theory that pike will move out of the reeds when the reeds are swaying in the wind. Whether this is true or false I cannot say, but it is a fact that the wind at least ruffles the surface of the water and provides some colour. These two factors are likely to help pike to feed.

Deep Dyke itself is a grand spot for bream during the nights and early mornings of summer and early autumn. There are one or two places where anglers can fish from the bank and it is quite rare for these not to be claimed.

Legering brings catches of as much as 100lb at a time to a rod, with bread the superior bait. For best results the swim should be heavily baited during the evening and fishing should begin an hour before dark.

In the middle of Deep Dyke, midway between Hickling and Heigham Sound, is Whiteslea, an area of shallow but open water. The reeds behind the open water conceal a network of dykes and small patches of water which hold numbers of bream and pike.

The Anglian Water Authority has leased the fishing from the Norfolk Naturalists' Trust and there is at present no charge to licence holders.

Horsey Mere

Horsey Mere, a broad in all but name, lies very close to the sea. In fact the silver sand dunes that mark the coastline can be seen from the mere. It is a remarkable water. For the short period of three years, 1966-68, it fished so well for pike that it was deservedly called the finest pike fishery in Britain.

In that time Peter Hancock caught his 40lb pike on a roach deadbait and Frank Wright, president of the Norwich and District AA, caught a 35-pounder on a spun deadbait. Other men caught pike topping the 30lb mark. It became known as an easy water. That may not have been strictly true, but anglers streamed to it from all parts of Britain and many of them caught their first-ever 20lb pike.

Typical was Caister publican Ron Clay who lived in Northampton at the time. Ron made his first visit to the mere, took one look at it and paused to make up his mind where he should begin fishing. He idly made a cast with a lure and seconds later was playing a big fish. He had caught a 26-pounder without really trying!

This phenomenal run of big pike was not destined to last long. In August 1969, the water in the mere became deoxygenated following a long period of drought, coupled with the pumping of dubious drainage water from the coastal marshes. At least 200 pike were collected and buried.

Opinions differ on the severity of the death roll, but I am of the opinion that all the pike in the mere died. Although some men continued to fish the mere, up to Christmas 1969 not one pike was caught after the mortality. The only known surviving pike within close distance of the mere were the small number of immature fish in the middle and

The Dennis Pye method of fishing a livebait in shallow water: 5ft or less. The float is two ¾ inch bored corks fixed to a peg. A livebait can tow this float around much easier than it could a traditional pike bung, with the result that it covers very much more ground and increases the chances of catching pike. There is normally no lead on the line, although in deeper water it could pay to use a minimum number of swan shot to keep the bait down near the bottom. A third and free-running bored cork can be allowed to run the line between the main float and the rod top. Thus when the main float is taken under the surface by a pike a visual guide remains on the surface to indicate the direction in which the pike is moving.

upper lengths of Waxham Cut.

This disaster, coupled with heavy losses on Hickling Broad and Heigham Sound, amounts to the greatest setback to Broadland fishing in living memory. But there is a brighter side — believe it or not. Horsey has lost its entire fish stock before. Just prior to the Second World War the sea broke through the coastal wall and flooded into the mere, wiping out the fish stocks. Within ten years it was fishing tolerably well again.

It was decided immediately after the losses were apparent that the area would not be restocked with pike. They would reappear of their own accord without assistance and the first priority was to rebuild the stocks of roach and bream. In effect the fishery authority did nothing to restore the losses.

Horsey was never worth a rating as a tench water but neither these fish nor the rudd that were once prolific – and weighing to over 30lb – have shown since the prymnesium outbreak. The perch had been lost before this problem arose.

Fortunately the roach and bream have made a relatively fast comeback. I have never rated Horsey as a bream water, putting it third best behind Heigham Sound and Hickling, but some excellent results were obtained in the summer of 1976.

The area close to the staithe can fish well at night or when boat traffic is light. Horsey does not suffer from boat traffic to the same extent as the middle Bure, for example, and the size of the mere is some guarantee of immunity from the worst of the traffic. The edge of the navigable channel to Waxham Cut will always produce its share of bream. I favour the section 300 yards into the broad. This was always an area where it was relatively easy to catch roach for livebaiting purposes and while catching roach I often contacted the bream. My catches were never heavy – for two reasons.

1. I was fishing for roach anyway and wasn't using enough groundbait to hold the shoal; and 2. this was always in the autumn when the bream tended to become less active.

The roach fishing can be most attractive. The stock contains a considerable number of fish topping 1lb and the average size of the fish caught on a single caster hookbait, fished on either a size 18 or 20 hook, can be higher than on some other broads.

Horsey's principal attraction has always been its pike fishing, however. I believe that by 1976 we were halfway through the inevitable bad time. There's nothing more certain than that Horsey will recover in full but this takes time. At least one 20lb pike has been caught there since the mass mortality. The small number of pike that survived in Waxham Cut would have been sufficient to provide the breeding nucleus and the stock is now increasing fast. It is still far short of the 1968 level but, always provided there are no more setbacks, sport should show a big improvement by 1980. Thereafter, if all goes well, we can expect the pike to reappear in something like their former numbers.

The average 20lb broads pike is from 10 to 12 years old. It figures that it must take that amount of time plus three years for the specimen pike to become numerous. Thirty-pounders will take a little longer but it is more than likely that some of the few survivors are now very big fish in their own right.

The fishing rights are owned by Mr. J.J. Buxton, of Horsey Hall, who told me the charges for pike fishing from the 1977 season would be £1 a day, 40p for roach and bream fishing. There is no fishing allowed in the period from 1 November to 1 February.

Martham Broad

The Thurne divides Martham and Somerton Broads, with reedbeds screening much of both waters from view of passing boats. Both are private and fishing is not allowed on them. In all there is a total of 60 acres of water, although this is made up of a chain of narrow bays rather than open sheets of water.

Most of the water is quite shallow but in both broads there are a number of small but appreciably deeper sections of up to $4\frac{1}{2}$ ft. These deeper holes are the prime holding ground for pike in winter, although the fish are also found out in the shallows when water temperature is higher.

Both waters lost what amounted to their entire stock in the prymnesium problem of 1969 but the return to normal is well underway. The pike are back in some strength but lack the size of the fish that formerly lived here. Some 20lb fish are there now and this breeding nucleus is important for future sport outside the broads themselves.

There is, regrettably, no indication that either the tench or rudd are reappearing. A great pity that, for the tench in particular helped maintain the stock in the nearby Thurne. A restocking with tench in this section of the Thurne could do much to restore the area as a whole but, despite high-sounding promises at the time, the fishery authority have been slow to do much that local anglers regard as constructive.

Although both these broads are private they perform a function as a sanctuary and are therefore of value to the fishery potential of the Upper Thurne.

Rockland Broad

Rockland Broad is the bigger of the two broads that drain into the River Yare – the other is Surlingham. Much of Rockland's water area is shallow but there has been extensive dredging of the channel to allow bigger motor cruisers to make passage across the broad to the village of Rockland St Mary and the New Inn.

The 50-acre broad is reputed to contain a fine stock of pike but it suffers from lack of attention by anglers. People who know it well insist there are 30lb pike there for the catching, but most fish live on this broad without having a bait offered to them.

Rockland Broad also holds plenty of bream – some of these are fish of better than 4lb, plenty of roach – with a high average weight – and a number of tench. Strange indeed that so many anglers should have so little interest in such potentially good fishing.

There is a 2ft rise and fall in the tide and a strong flow runs through the connecting dyke to the Yare. For this reason anglers on larger boats have to take care. Mooring in the shallows at high water can mean the boat will become stuck fast on the mud with no hope of relief until the next high tide.

The deeper part of the broad is at the north end and this and the boat channel are the best prospects for the roach. Fishing boats can be hired in Rockland St Mary.

Oulton Broad

The excessive commercial use of Oulton Broad has taken its toll in recent years. Throughout the summer the surface is one constant turmoil of holiday craft and the anglers inevitably comes off second best. Oulton has though a great reputation for quality fish, mainly for its perch, but the bream can be good, the roach better than average and the pike numerous, if not record-busters.

The perch have taken a knock. There was a time when the broad was worth at least one 4-pounder every year, with a succession of supporting fish weighing better than 3lb. The best on record for the water is the 4lb 12oz perch by the late Sid Baker, of Norwich, the fish that holds the British national record. Second best is a fish of 4lb $9\frac{1}{2}$ oz by Lowestoft angler Les Proudfoot.

All of this seems far away. The perch suffered a virtual

wipe-out in the mid-1960s and fish of 3lb haven't been taken since. This is a national as well as a local tragedy, for Oulton was without question the finest big perch water in the country. It was consistent and the perch were big. There was always an ample head of small fish growing into big ones and it hardly seemed possible this decline could set in.

Fortunately the worst is over. No matter how many fish die from whatever cause, there always seem to be sufficient remaining to repair the damage ... but it takes time. Ten years have passed since the water was denuded and the little perch are starting to show up again. As yet they appear to have a top weight of 8oz but they are growing and the 4-pounders will show again just as soon as the fish have had sufficient time to grow to that weight.

Statistics show that the perch used to be caught all over the broad. There was a chance of a specimen almost everywhere and this happy situation must make a comeback. Undoubtedly the best area though was Carlton Ham, the big bay immediately above the Yacht Station. Lots of boats are at permanent anchor in this bay and perch find such areas irresistible. They love to feed on and under boats and this could perhaps be why they were always attracted to this bay.

Other areas that used to produce their share of the specimen perch crop included the water close to Mutford Lock at the Wherry Hotel, close to the Malthouse and in the dead end dyke where most of the boatyards are to be found. The dead end of the dyke often produced its best fish late in the season after the first of the frosts had induced the hordes of small roach to flock into the upper limits of the dyke.

When the perching was in its heyday all acknowledged methods produced the fish. Some of the specimens came on float-fished worms, other on livebait and more on spinners. But many of the anglers who fished here came specifically for the perch and they tended to concentrate on livebait and lure fishing so worms don't figure so high in the ratings.

The two biggest fish were both caught on livebait, but Les Proudfoot has a perch of 4lb 5oz on a small vibrating spoon. The biggest disadvantage with worms was that they attracted large numbers of the smaller fish, whereas lures and livebaits were more selective.

Local anglers always had the best results and they preferred to use single hook tackle for their livebaits. The sea angler's dab hook mounted on extra-strong nylon hook lengths was their favourite. That strong hook length was often necessary since the broad does hold fair numbers of pike and these could be a nuisance, chopping through finer nylon with ease when they took baits intended for perch.

Fortunately the pike were not at their most numerous in the areas formerly dominated by perch. Occasional double figure pike are taken out of Carlton Ham, I got one myself while fishing for perch... and a 3lb 10oz perch! Generally though the biggest catches of pike are made in North Bay, on the right-hand side of the broad towards Oulton Dyke. These fish show best early in the pike season, with October and November having the best form.

The pike are usually close to the reed beds – even right inside the beds – and that explains why low water is rated the best time to catch them. As the level drops to its lowest point the water leave the reeds and the pike have to move out into the open water, where they are more vulnerable to anglers' baits. Local clubs have found that they catch four pike in the low water hour for every one they take in the remainder of the tide phase.

No-one has been able to give a satisfactory reason for the pike's preference for this section of broad. Perhaps it is sufficient for our needs that we should know this is the case, but tagging experiments highlighted the point. A number of pike caught in local club pike contests were taken to the Yacht Station for weighing in, tagged and returned alive. Those same fish later returned to the North Bay area.

The best pike ever taken off Oulton weighed $27\frac{1}{2}$ lb. There have been others over 20lb but no-one would claim this is the best pike fishery around. It's good for fish up to 15lb but it was never remotely comparable with Horsey Mere when Horsey was in top form.

The bream have proved rather more elusive in recent years. There are some dense shoals on the broad but they seem to have more than their fair share of wanderlust, never settling for long in one place in summer. The one predictable bream area is Oulton Dyke, at the head of the broad and linking with the Waveney. After spawning on the broad proper the bream move into the dyke, perhaps preferring the stronger flow evident there. Even the dyke hasn't been quite on its best behaviour recently but this does present the best chance of a 50lb total.

The broad's roach have improved. At one time there were too many of them for their own good. They never really seemed to grow as big as we would have liked. But once the numbers were reduced the survivors and their subsequent progeny grew bigger and faster on the basis, presumably, that the fewer fish there are the more food there is for each one. The roach are widespread throughout, although the bigger ones are not always easy to locate, some of the best catches being made on caster. From time to time anglers who have set their stalls out for roach have cheerfully settled for a catch of bream after these fish have moved in.

The broad has a hard bottom and averages around 6ft in depth — rather more than some of the Norfolk Broads. This isn't really suitable for tench and these fish have never been present in any numbers worth mentioning.

So, at the moment Oulton is at an in between stage. It hasn't fished really well for ten years but it must come back to rival its best. The roach are the most predictable at present but expect the perch to show in 1980, with regular catches of big fish becoming more common a year or two thereafter.

If that seems a long time to have to wait, be assured there are lots of anglers who eagerly await the return of those days when the big perch were the main attraction and everything else was a sideshow.

Ormesby Broads

The landlocked broads of the Ormesby groups are some of the most attractive in all of Broadland but most visitors to the area never see them at all. They are cut off from the main river system except for a small dyke known as Muck Fleet that flows into the Bure below Acle. Navigation up this dyke is not possible.

The Ormesby group consists of individual sections: Ormesby, Filby, Rollesby and Lily. Each is a broad in its own right but the waters are really all one, divided only by bridges and narrow straits. Together they cover an area of some 800 acres. The broads are generally deep by local standards with much of their water being at least 10ft deep and containing odd holes running to 16ft.

There is no bank fishing, except in the tiny corners where boats are available for hire. The banks are reed-fringed and unapproachable overland. The deeper water is usually in the middle of the wide expanses and best results are made close to the reeds, where the water is shallower, but by casting out towards the open water.

It is for bream and pike that the broads are principally known, for the roach, although extremely numerous, are very small and 1lb fish almost unknown. There are some rudd, mainly found in the shallow edges in summer, but these are not so numerous as on some other broads.

The bream stock suffered a setback four years ago and

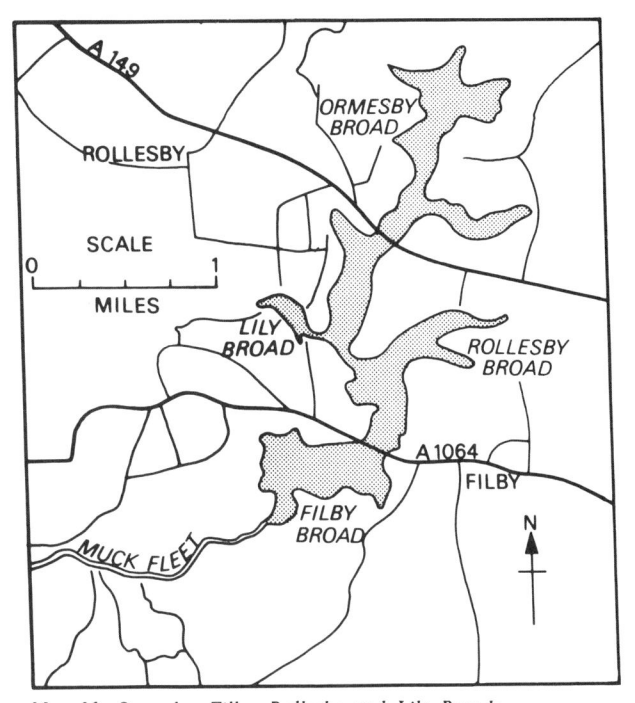

Map 11. Ormesby, Filby, Rollesby and Lily Broads

large numbers of fish died. The cause was some type of algal pollution. The water became exceptionally coloured, remained like that for a long period and then suddenly reverted to gin clear. In the period of gin-clear water sport was extremely poor and anglers tended to take the pessimistic view that the bream had suffered a near wipe-out. Pike were just about the only fish to be caught at that time.

The 1975 and 1976 seasons showed considerable improvement. The fish do not even now appear to have regained their former numbers but quantities of smaller ones are beginning to show again and, given time, the eternal healer, all will be well again.

True to form the surviving big bream have shown themselves to be very big indeed. Whereas fish of 5lb were rated exceptional before the stock was thinned, fish caught since have been much bigger. In the summer of 1976 three bream over 8lb were caught – one of these topped 9lb and on that basis the 1980s must produce some bream over the 10lb mark.

Once the bream come back in full strength the size of the biggest fish is likely to reduce once more. This is the normal pattern in a constantly changing situation.

The bream are a better prospect in summer. They are rarely caught in the winter. Without any doubt the favourite time to catch the big fish feeding is from first light until mid-morning. There is almost always a mid-day lull followed by more sport in the last two hours of daylight.

Heavy groundbaiting is essential. Anglers who turn up to fish with a couple of 1lb bags of groundbait are unlikely to get the best from their fishing. I recommend that anglers bait a swim very heavily in late evening and return to it to fish at first light next day. At that time they can expect the bream to feed fast and furiously until around 9.30 am when sport begins to ease — and often comes to an abrupt halt.

The tench have never been numerous but there are enough of them to provide an unexpected bonus to the day's fishing... and a 6-pounder is a possibility.

If anglers intend to fish these broads for a period of several days so much the better. They should keep to the same swims each day, always groundbaiting heavily at the end of the day to attract the bream during the night. It is a great pity that all the fishing boats have to be back at their moorings at night. If only anglers were allowed to fish right through the hours of darkness bream catches would be astronomical, but they are not allowed to fish at night and early morning is the next best thing.

The bream can be caught on all the recognized baits — bread flake and paste, maggots and worm — but bread is almost always best. A size 10 hook baited with a piece the size of a man's thumbnail is ideal. Personally I prefer flake to paste but some of the heaviest catches have been made on paste.

As with most waters of this type the very best results come during the warmer spells of weather and if the temperature has been high for several weeks without a break then propects are perfect. A light breeze ruffling the surface is also useful.

One snag is that the broads are heavily populated with grebe. These fish-eating birds think nothing of invading a swim anglers are fishing and they will dive into groundbaited areas and catch fish. This, of course, is hardly helpful.

All broads here have a good reputation for pike and it is a poor season that does not produce at least one fish topping the 20lb mark. In recent years anglers fishing with legered herring have done very well, taking large numbers of pike over 10lb. At times pike can be found in groups and anglers who catch one fish can reasonably expect to catch more from the same spot. I have found that it pays to fish on for half an hour in any swim that has produced one pike, for there are almost certain to be more fish near by. The biggest catches of pike are usually made in areas not too distant from reed-beds. For that reason it can often be time wasted to spend too long in the middle of the broads.

Boats are available for hire at the Eel's Foot Hotel and from Alexander's at Ormesby and at Ormesby St Michael and Filby. It pays to book in advance.

Fritton Lake

There's no denying that traffic-free fisheries are at a premium in East Anglia — which makes Fritton Lake of greater importance than might otherwise be the case. The lake isn't completely landlocked. It is connected to the Waveney at St. Olaves by an overflow stream called Blocka Run but there is no motorized boat traffic on the lake and the stream is not navigable. Fritton is some six miles from the coast and is situated equal distances from Lowestoft and Great Yarmouth.

The lake covers 170 acres, much of it more than 10ft and extending to 17ft deep, but there are also shallow areas containing lily beds in summer. The stock is varied but bream are the primary species. The roach are small fish in the main, there are many pike, and a long term carp stock has been augmented as recently as 1975.

In common with a number of other stillwaters — the Ormesby group of broads, for example — Fritton's bream have grown bigger in recent years than they have been known to previously. Fritton's bream always topped 5lb but in the summer of 1976 a number of really big fish to 7lb 8oz were caught.

The small bream don't show very often and big catches are almost always made up with really hefty fish. The biggest one-day catch recorded in the summer of 1976 was of 400lb, shared by two men in one boat. The sample in this catch was quite exceptional. The weighed from 5lb to 7lb 4oz each. All were caught on bread flake.

Many of the bigger catches are taken boat fishing but shore angling also produces its share of the bream. Fritton has generous bank fishing space which at the time of writing provided 80 anglers at any one time. Bank clearing and improvement work underway in 1976 and to be continued into 1977 is expected to increase the area available into space for over 100 anglers. Some of the shore fishing is from specially-built wooden stagings.

The best bream catches come during periods of warm weather. Fritton fishes best over amply groundbaited swims and anglers who fish for just a single day often miss out with the heavyweight catches.

It pays to feed one swim heavily and stick with it. Bream browse the lake bed in much the same way that cattle graze a meadow, so, give them enough time and they will eventually turn up. If the water temperature is to their liking the bream will move on to the groundbait and clear it up before moving on. Give them enough and they will stay rooted to that area... and that's how the big catches are made.

Once the bream are firmly established on a well-baited patch they will continue to feed through the day but early mornings are favourite. There is always a strong temptation to move to another spot elsewhere in a lake if the first day has proved to be average or worse. This should be resisted at Fritton. Stick with the original swim, feed it again and rely on the fish turning up.

It's easy to move to a second site only for the bream to have moved to the first swim. It may sometimes be sensible to chase shoals of rudd but it is rather pointless if bream are the quarry. Stay and wait and eventually anglers will be rewarded by far bigger catches.

Maggots and worm will catch bream in the coloured water which shows in mid-summer but bread paste has proved to be far and away the best bait – both for aggregate catches and for the bigger fish.

The carp have never really given a good account of themselves. The stock must include fish well in excess of 20lb but these continue to be most elusive. A carp fishing specimen hunter could enjoy himself here in the knowledge that he would have to earn his success but that he might turn up something really spectacular.

Oddly enough anglers haven't seen the best of the pike fishing either. I am prepared to think that fish running very close, even over the 30lb mark, are there for the catching but the biggest caught recently were short of 20lb.

There is a fleet of 25 fishing boats available for hire and club contests are catered for. The daily hire charge for a boat is £1.50, £1.00 for a half-day. In addition there is a daily fishing ticket costing 50p, but this entitles its buyer to fish from any of the shore stations. The daily fishing charge for juniors is 30p.

Advance bookings and additional information is available from W. Mussett, Fritton Old Hall (telephone Fritton 208), who can also advise on holiday accommodation close by.

Lakes and Pits

BLICKLING LAKE: An excellent water situated near Aylsham. It contains large numbers of bream and tench and these species provide the best fishing. There are also pike and rudd in the 20 acre water. The fishing is leased by the Anglian Water Authority and can be fished on a day permit costing 25 pence. The bailiff collects.

The lake is quiet and secluded and offers one of the few motor boat-free waters in the area. It is popular throughout the summer but huge lengths of the bank provide comfortable fishing and this is an ideal place to take the family. Row boats can be hired for boat fishing.

HAVERINGLAND LAKE: This 12 acre lake contains some very big pike with numerous bream and good numbers of tench. Some carp. The water is often very clear which tends to make fishing difficult but this is a water where anglers seeking big fish will enjoy the challenge. The deepest water is at the dam end, where it measures up to 8ft.

HOLKHAM LAKE: Situated near Wells, this excellent tench water contain fish to 6lb, together with roach and dace. The roach fishing was once voted fabulous but is not yet back at its best. A fertile fishery containing massive weed beds, it is the best prospect in the North Norfolk area for anglers holidaying by the sea who want to be reasonably sure of some sport.

No Sunday fishing and is otherwise open only from June 15 to the end of August. Day tickets from the estate office at Holkham.

LENWADE LAKES: An excellent tench, pike, roach and bream fishery, about 10 miles north west of Norwich. Controlled by the London Anglers' Association. There are five lakes in this group and they collectively rank with the best waters of their type. Tench have been caught to 6lb 12oz, and the bream are equally big. The pike do not appear to be big but rudd top 12lb. A day ticket water. The bailiff collects.

MARTHAM PITS: This chain of small pits is located close to the River Thurne on the upstream side of Martham Ferry. The water is clear and heavily weeded in summer but contains some well above average size tench. Fish weighing close to 7lb have been caught. There are also some pike, bream and roach.

It is a difficult water in which to obtain results and its big fish tally would probably be much higher if fishing was allowed through the night. But the pits are not navigable so they offer quiet undisturbed fishing through the day. A charge is made for the fishing and this is collected by the bailiff on his rounds.

Fishing Tackle Dealers

AYLSHAM: C. Clarke, 30 Market Place
BECCLES: A. Crack, 7 Blyburgate
CAISTER: I.R. Flaxman, 3 Tan Lane
CROMER: Marine Sports, 21 New Street
EAST DEREHAM: H.C. Fanthorpe, 5 Norwich Street
FAKENHAM: Len Bryer, Rear Pooley, Norwich Street
GORLESTON: Baker and O'Keefe, 7 Pier Walk
    E.K. & E. Edwards, 16 Quayside
GREAT YARMOUTH: F.C. Pownall, 74 Regent Road
    J.I. Markham, 43 South Market Road
    R. Davies, 26 South Market Road
HARLESTON: G. Denny & Sons Ltd., Market Place
HORNING: Nando's, Lower Street
LOWESTOFT: S.G. Hook, 132 Bevan Street
    E. Bean, 175 London Road North
NORWICH: A.C. Browne & Son, 6 Timber Hill
    T. Stevenson Ltd., Swan Lane
    Peter Roach, 54 St. Augustine's Street
    Thorpe Electrical and Cycle Co., 14/16 Plumstead Road East
    Gale and Galey Ltd., 75 Prince of Wales Road
    Tom Boulton, 173 Drayton Road
    Gallyon's, Bedford Street
    John Wilson, Bridewell Alley
    T. Allen, 168 Silver Road
NORTH WALSHAM: R.H. Webb, 28 Market Place
OULTON BROAD: A.A. Collen & Son, 17 Commodore Road
POTTER HEIGHAM: Bridge Stores, (Potter Heigham) Ltd.
    Ken Latham, Latham's Stores
SHERINGHAM: Marine Sports, 19 Station Road
WROXHAM: Roys (Wroxham) Ltd., Hardware Department
    G. Haylett, Station Road

Fishing Boats for Hire

BARTON TURF: Cox Bros., The Staithe (telephone Smallburgh 206)

HICKLING: Whispering Reeds boatyard (telephone Hickling 314)

HORNING: New Inn (telephone Horning 309)

LUDHAM: Ludham Marine Ltd., Womack Staithe (telephone St. Benets 322)

IRSTEAD: Barton Angler Hotel (telephone Horning 727)

NORWICH: Norwich and District Angling Association, C. Braithwaite, 4 Cranage Road (telephone Norwich 25682)

MARTHAM: Martham Ferry Boatyard (telephone Martham 303)

Martham Building and Development Company (telephone Martham 249)

Len Spencer (telephone Martham 352)

ORMESBY: The Eel's Foot (telephone Great Yarmouth 730217)

OULTON BROAD: A.A. Collen, 17 Commodore Road (telephone Lowestoft 4811)

POTTER HEIGHAM: Herbert Woods (telephone Potter Heigham 711)

W. May (telephone Potter Heigham 241)

WROXHAM: E.C. Burton, 'Merton', Hoveton (telephone Wroxham 2751)

Jack Powles & Co. Ltd., (telephone Wroxham 2101)

J. Loynes & Sons (telephone Wroxham 2232)

Note: some of the above have day launches, others rowing and outboard motor equipped craft for hire.

Day-boats and rowing boats can be hired from most of the boatyards mainly concerned with the weekly holiday trade. Although casual callers can often obtain a boat, it pays to obtain reservations in advance. Most of the firms supplying motor cruisers and yachts are members of booking agencies. These are: Blakes (Norfolk Broads Holidays) Ltd., Stalham Road, Hoveton, Wroxham, Norfolk (telephone Wroxham 2141) Hoseasons, Sunway House, Oulton Broad (telephone Lowestoft 64991). In addition both Blakes and Hoseasons have many chalets, caravans and bungalows for hire both on the riverside and by the sea.

Index

Acle 32
Aldeby 59
Ant, River 33 - 9
Ant Mouth 30, 31
Arminghall 51 - 2
Attlebridge 66
Aylsham 19

Barford 43
Barnby 59
Barsham 58
Barton Broad 74 - 6
Bawburgh 43, 44
Beauchamp Arms 50
Beccles 58 - 9
Belaugh 22
Bintry mill 64
Black Swan Inn (Waveney) 55
Blickling Lake 97
Boat House Hill 59
Bramerton 48
Bridge Broad (Wroxham) 22, 25
Bridge Lakes (Lenwade) 66
Briggate Lock 33
Brockdish 54
Brundall 49
Buck Hills 55
Buckenham 49 - 50
Bungay 55 - 6
Bure, River 19 - 33
Burgh 19 - 20
Burgh St Peter 59, 60
Buxton Mill 20

Candle Dyke 42
Cantley 50
Chedgrave 51
Chet, River 51
Church Dyke 46
City New Mills (Norwich) 68
Clacton marshes 50
Colney 44, 45
Coltishall Common 22
Costessey Mill 67
Cringleford 45

Daisy Broad 22, 24
Deep Dyke (Hickling) 80, 84, 85
Didler's Mill 28
Dilham Cut 34

Dolphin Bridge (Norwich) 68
Drayton 67

Earlham 44
Earsham 55
Ellingham 52
Ellingham Mill 56
Elsing Mill 65

Fakenham 63
Ferry Inn (Horning) 29, 30
Filby Broad 92
Fishers Row 61
Flixton 55
Forncett 52
Foundry bridge (Norwich) 68
Fritton Lake 95 - 6

Geldeston 56 - 7
Great Witchingham Lakes (Lenwade) 66
Guist 63 - 4

Haddiscoe 61
Haveringland Lake 97
Heigham Sound 76 - 82
Hellesdon Mill 67
Hickling Broad 82 - 5
High's Mill 42
Holkham Lake 97
Homersfield bridge 55
Honing 33, 34
Horning 28 - 30
Horsey Mere 85 - 8
Horstead 19, 20, 22
Hoveton Great Broad 28
Hoveton Little Broad 28, 72 - 3
How Hill 37
Hoxne 53
Hunset Mill 36

Irstead 36 - 7

Keswick 45
King's Dyke 20

Langley 50
Lenwade 66
Lenwade Lakes 97

101

Lily Broad 92
Loddon 51
Ludham Bridge 38
Lyng Mill 65

Malthouse Broad 73
Marlingford 43, 44
Martham Broad 88
Martham Ferry 42
Martham Pits 97 8
Mayton bridge 20
Meadow Dyke (Horsey) 80
Mendham Bridge 54

Needham Mill 54
New Cut (Haddiscoe) 61
Newton Flotman 52
North Elmham 64
Norwich 67 - 8

Ormesby Broads 92 - 5
Oulton Broad 89 - 92
Oulton Dyke 59, 61
Oxnead 20

Pleasure Boat Inn (Hickling) 83, 84
Postwick 48
Potter Heigham 41, 42

Ranworth Dyke 73
Reedham 50
Repps 41
Ringland 66
Rockland Broad 89
Rollesby Broad 92
Ryburgh 63 - 4

St Benet's Abbey 31
Salhouse Broad 27, 70 - 2
Salhouse Little Broad 26
Scole 52, 53
Sennowe Park Lake 64

Shotesham 52
Shotford Bridge 54
Somerton Broad 42
South Walsham Broads 74
South Walsham Dyke 31
Stalham Dyke 36
Station Lakes (Lenwade) 66
Stokesby 33
Stracey Arms 33
Strumpshaw 48, 49
Surlingham 48
Sutton Broad 36
Swan Hotel (Horning) 28, 29
Swanton Morley 64 - 5
Syleham 54

Tas, River 51 - 2
Taverham 66
Thorpe Green 47
Thurne, River 39 - 43
Thurne Mouth 41, 42
Tonnage Bridge 34
Trowse Mill 45, 46

Upton 31 - 2

Wainford 56
Waveney, River 52 - 61
Wayford Bridge 34 - 6
Wensum, River 61 - 9
Wensum Park 67
Weybread Pits 54
Whiteslea (Hickling) 85
Whitlingham 47
Womack Dyke 41 - 2
Woodbastwick Decoy Broad 72
Woodbastwick Staithe 28
Worlingham Mill 59
Wroxham 22 - 5
Wroxham Broad 25, 69 - 70

Yare, River 43 - 50

Set by Johel Typesetters Ltd and printed in Great Britain by The Anchor Press, Tiptree, Essex.